Medieval Craft and Mystery

Discovering the People behind York's Mystery Plays

CONTENTS

Foreword

York's famous cycle of Mystery Plays was first performed in the late 14th century, a time when the city was enjoying great economic prosperity as the administrative centre of the north of England. One of the most significant contributions to this successful economy was made by the city's craftspeople, many of whom were members of craft guilds, organisations made up of men (and some women) who broadly carried out the same jobs. The guilds played an important role in the life of the city, providing not only goods and services essential to everyday life, but also helping to meet the needs of their members, both those in work and those no longer in employment. Just as importantly, they were responsible each year for the funding, producing and performing of their own particular play of the play cycle.

Although we know them as 'The Mystery Plays', this term is not one that the citizens of medieval York would have used. It is, in fact, a fairly recently invented name, which makes use of two meanings of the word 'mystery'. The craft guilds, and the skilled crafts of their members, were known as mysteries. Mystery also has a theological meaning, as in a mystical religious truth. The plays were actually a series of pageants, dramatising stories from the Old and New Testaments, starting with the Fall of the Angels and the Creation, and concluding with the Last Judgment. Each pageant was 'brought forth' by a different guild, or collection of guilds, and together these were known as the 'Corpus Christi play', because it was performed in association with the feast of Corpus Christi. This was celebrated on the first Thursday after Trinity Sunday, a date which fell in the mid-summer period of 23 May–24 June.

We can learn a great deal about the lives of York's artisans from surviving documentary records of the time; these tell us how the guilds originated and how they functioned, and also about the Mystery Plays and how they were performed. Increasingly, however, archaeology has been providing us with a different type of evidence – the physical remains of places where these men and women lived, worked and met together, the tools they used, and the products they made. This has been gathered from 40 years of excavations and research across the city, from sites large and small, some very well known, and others less so. By exploring this archaeological knowledge and combining it with insights from historical documents, it is possible to bring some of the original performers of medieval York's Mystery Plays to life.

The Craft Guilds

Origins

The craft guild system appears to have developed from the desire of artisans involved in the same occupations to provide support systems for their co-workers; these offered both social and spiritual support, including financial support to those who had fallen on hard times, and celebrating annual masses for the dead. These associations, which may have emerged as early as the 13th century and were often allied to religious fraternities, began to develop systems of self-regulation for their crafts. These might include rules about the employment of apprentices, the levels of wages, where and at what times of day work was to be carried out, and from whom their raw materials should be bought. To be a member of the guild and to carry on a trade as a master, it was necessary to be a 'freeman'; this gave the freedom to trade without hindrance in the city and to be a full citizen, with voting rights. Freedom would be purchased from the city; in 1502, for example, an apprentice had to pay £1 for his freedom, while the son of a freeman paid only 1 shilling. For others the charge was £2.

A copper-alloy seal matrix belonging to Robert the Clockmaker, who may have been a smith, found in excavations at Low Petergate

Functions

The regulations of the guilds which related to working practices were recorded in their ordinances; these were designed to offer some protection from increasing local, national and even international competition. Officers of the guilds varied in number and character from one craft to another, but all included at least two searchers who were responsible for maintaining standards of workmanship amongst the members of their guild. Their responsibilities included summoning meetings of the guild; managing its finances; 'searching' or checking the quality of their members' products, as well as those being imported into the city by 'foreigners' (anyone from outside the city); approving new members and regulating the taking on of apprentices. Other officers might include a master of the guild, as well as pageant-masters, who had overall responsibility for the annual Corpus Christi Day performances by their guild. All the officers were elected annually by the members.

The ordinances of the guilds were registered and endorsed by the city authorities, which meant that the guild officers were responsible to both the guild and the city council. The mayor could demand guild meetings should be held, and enforce discipline between guilds in conflict with each other. Income from fines imposed under the ordinances would be shared between the city and the guild.

The widespread view that the customer was of utmost importance encouraged an emphasis on the quality of workmanship and of raw materials; when shoddy goods or faulty work was revealed by searches, offenders were sent to the mayor for punishment. Rules were also devised to ensure consumers were not subject to harassment by members who might be overly keen to offer their services or products. In order to protect their members' interests, attempts were made to ensure

Lead-alloy cloth seals, denoting the quality of finished cloth (found at Judge's Lodging, Lendal; Skeldergate, Pawson's Warehouse)

guild monopolies; an area around York was sometimes defined in which only craftsmen from the city could sell their products. Other guilds insisted that their craft skills should not be taught to outsiders for financial gain, or that no one from outside the guild should be employed by its members. Ultimately, many of these protectionist strategies failed; it was impossible for a guild to prohibit everyone outside its membership from performing the same jobs as those within, and distinctions between guilds were often blurred. This latter issue frequently led to disagreements. The smiths, for example, found themselves in dispute with the cutlers over the manufacture of edged tools and blades. The barkers (leather tanners) and cordwainers (shoe-makers) maintained long-running disagreements over the supply and quality of tanned leather, with the cordwainers successfully petitioning the council in the 15th century to be allowed to 'search' or examine the quality of tanned leather. An outbreak of physical violence by the barkers over the decision to put together a committee of members of four different guilds to examine leather led to them being denied the right to search leather at all for a brief time.

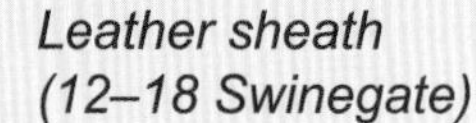

Leather sheath (12–18 Swinegate)

Leather offcuts from a workshop (College of the Vicars Choral, Bedern)

Over the course of the medieval period, the guilds varied in their membership numbers, all being affected by economic conditions. Some guilds chose to work together for the purposes of the pageants, but there were also full amalgamations between certain allied crafts. Sometimes this may have been an economic necessity, and was presumably the result of an agreement that it would be in the interests of both parties; this may have been the case with the pinners' guild, which merged with the wiredrawers, who were the suppliers of the wire used in pin-making. Sometimes it may have resulted from the taking over of a smaller less powerful craft by a larger one. Sheathers, for example, made leather sheaths, and appear in the early 15th century to have issued their own craft ordinances, but by 1445 the cutlers' ordinances indicate that the sheathers, bladesmiths and cutlers were all part of the same craft.

Some crafts, such as masons, never had guilds. Masons often took their skills wherever they were required, so they would expect to move from project to project, and place to place. A master mason would be appointed on a salary for the length of the project to oversee the work of the craftsmen who were paid weekly. Lodges would be established on large building sites with a master mason in charge, not answerable to the city authorities. A city such as York with institutions such as the Minster would have provided constant work for masons, so there may well have been a permanent body of such men, but there is no record that there was ever a masons' guild in York.

Architectural fragment, Hungate

Religious guilds

In addition to craft guilds, there were also purely religious guilds, of which the Corpus Christi guild was the largest and wealthiest. Membership of these guilds included clergy as well as craftsmen already belonging to craft guilds; these guilds had spiritual and compassionate aims, seeking to care for their members, but also helping the sick and infirm in the wider society. The Corpus Christi guild was not established until the 15th century, some time after the custom of performing pageants in association with the feast of Corpus Christi had originated, but it seems that the guild was involved with the organisation of the civic procession rather than the pageants themselves.

Today's guilds

In 1415 there were 96 craft guilds in York – today there are seven. The Gild of Freemen is the city's oldest guild, dating back to the mid-1100s, when they were the only people allowed to trade within the city; today there are thought to be approximately 5000 freemen of York. The Company of Cordwainers, which was dissolved in 1808–09, was revived in 1977 by members of the shoe trade, while The York Guild of Building was established in 1954, and incorporates many of the building trades which originally had their own individual guilds. All three of these guilds use Bedern Hall for their meetings, although this particular hall was originally the refectory (dining hall) for the College of the Vicars Choral, rather than a guildhall. The Company of the Merchant Taylors and The Company of the Merchant Adventurers have their own guildhalls in which to meet.

Bedern Hall

Finally, the Guild of Scriveners was revived in 1981, and has its base at Clifton Moor Business Park, and the Company of Butchers was reconstituted in 1941; the latter is based at Jacob's Well in Trinity Lane, Micklegate.

Archaeology and the guilds

Excavations

Although it is possible to illustrate the work of many of the craftsmen by the tools which they used and the products they created, the physical remains of others do not survive. We have no archaeological evidence relating to members of guilds such as the hosiers (makers of breeches and leggings), or the chandlers (candle-makers) for example, as their products do not survive burial in the ground, and the precise tools that they used are unknown; unfortunately this is also true of other crafts. Archaeological evidence of where craft working was carried out is also hard to find, as the occasionally recovered tool, or small amount of working debris most typically found in excavations, is not sufficient evidence of activity on the site itself; many types of craft will have left no structural traces either. Some sites where working appears to have been undertaken have been identified, however.

A late 15th–early 16th century hearth and working floor uncovered at the Bedern Foundry excavation

One activity that tends to more easily identified than others, probably because its physical remains tend to be robust and consequently survive well, is metalworking. Large-scale excavations in the 1970s in the area of Bedern revealed the presence of a foundry operating in the 13th–early 16th centuries; the foundations of a number of industrial buildings were identified, as were hearths and furnaces constructed of tiles and bricks, working floors and casting pits. The finds indicated that copper-alloy vessels

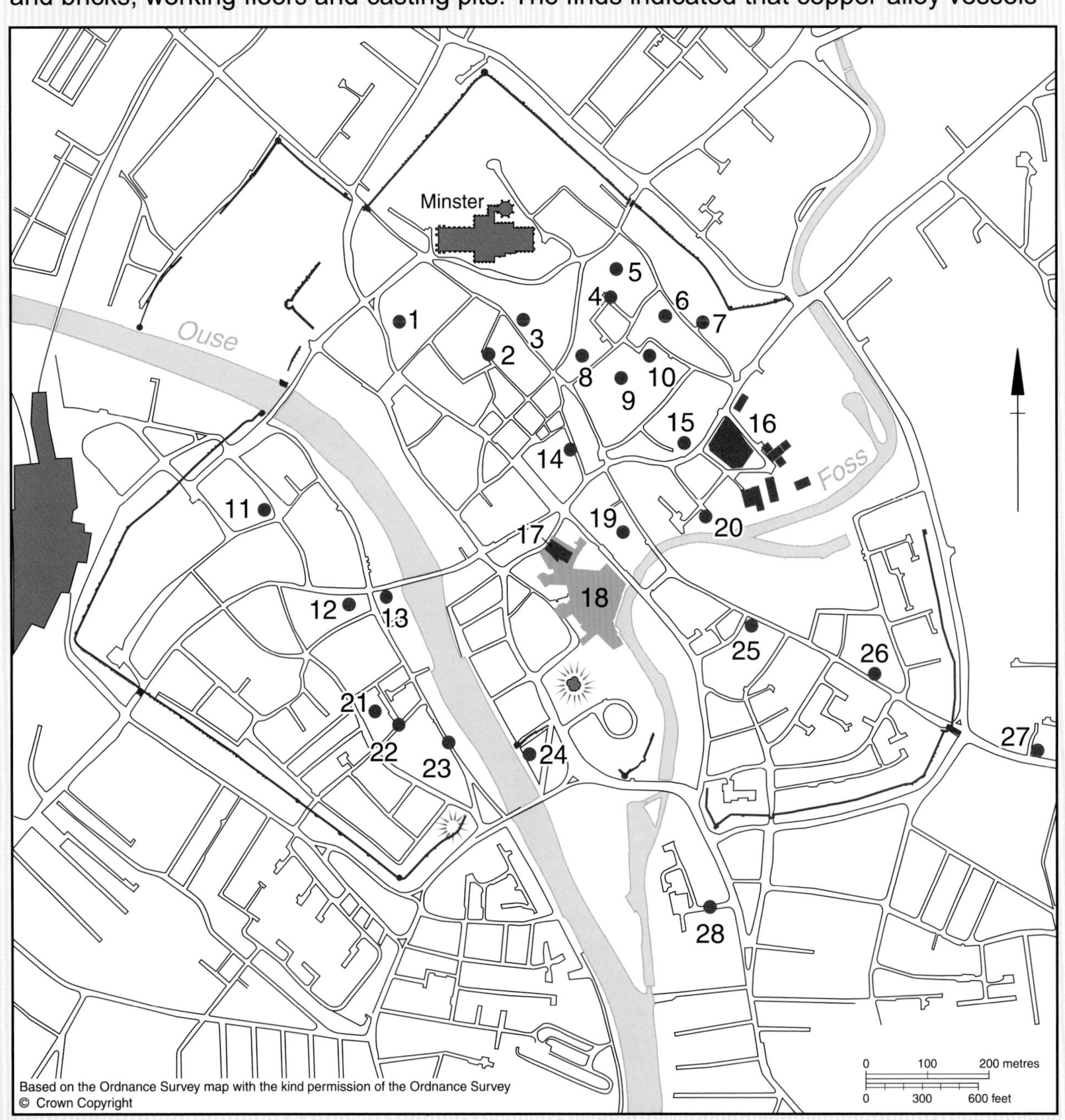

such as cauldrons, and small dress accessories were being cast there, but church bells may also have been products. The evidence of small-scale ironsmithing on the site was interpreted as possibly resulting from the making of tools for the foundry. In the 1990s, excavations nearby in St Andrewgate and Spen Lane found further evidence of the casting of copper-alloy dress fittings in the area in the early 14th–early 16th centuries. Structural features included hearths and working floors, sites for anvils, and quenching pits, with concentrations of metalworking debris such as slag and hammerscale also present. Workshop areas seem to have been located at the rear of the properties, which may have had a shop front on the street, as well as living areas for the metalworkers and their families.

The redevelopment of the former York College for Girls at 62–68 Low Petergate led to excavations in 2004–2005; here several different crafts appeared to have been carried out in adjoining tenements. Both remains of related structures, including furnaces and kilns, and finds such as slag and mould fragments were recovered, suggesting ironworking and copper-alloy working had been happening here, though not necessarily at the same time. The other crafts identified were horn-working and leather-working, probably cobbling, that is the repair of shoes, rather than cordwaining (shoe manufacture). Nearby in the Swinegate area, excavations in the late 1980s and early 1990s similarly produced evidence of copper-alloy working and associated workshops. Away from this area of the city, a complex of timber-framed buildings recognised in excavations at 41–49 Walmgate in 2000 revealed an iron smithy with a contemporary copper-alloy vessel casting operation, both situated within a complex of timber-framed

Facing page: Map of York showing excavations mentioned in the text

1. *9 Blake Street*
2. *12–18 Swinegate*
3. *62–68 Low Petergate*
4. *The College of Vicars Choral at Bedern*
5. *Bedern Foundry*
6. *30 Aldwark*
7. *Ebor Brewery, 21–33 Aldwark*
8. *71–73 Goodramgate*
9. *Land off St Andrewgate/Spen Lane*
10. *St Andrewgate*
11. *24–30 Tanner Row*
12. *Queen's Hotel, 1–9 Micklegate*
13. *1–9 Bridge Street*
14. *34 Shambles*
15. *The former Henlys Garage, Stonebow*
16. *Hungate*
17. *16–22 Coppergate*
18. *Coppergate Watching Brief*
19. *Merchant Adventurers' Hall*
20. *Carmelite Street*
21. *37 Bishophill Senior*
22. *58–59 Skeldergate*
23. *City Mills, Skeldergate*
24. *1–2 Tower Street*
25. *41–49 Walmgate*
26. *118–126 Walmgate*
27. *27 Lawrence Street*
28. *46–54 Fishergate*

Excavation of the tenements at 62–68 Low Petergate

buildings and workshops, dating from the mid-14th to the late 16th century. The evidence suggested that living and working quarters were in close proximity and that at times there may have been a shop on the Walmgate street frontage.

Elsewhere in the city, hints at possible craft-working are mainly provided by the artefacts or other material culture. The presence of abundant bark fragments at a site on Layerthorpe Bridge, for example, is thought to indicate tanning activity on the site, while unusually large numbers of sheep bones, specifically foot bones, found in a 15th century cess pit at 58–59 Skeldergate have been interpreted as debris from the processing of sheepskins, also known as 'tawing'; the feet were left attached for ease of handling during the pegging out of the skin.

At the site of the former Henlys Garage on Stonebow, copper-alloy chain mail links made of wire were found, which appeared to have been discarded during manufacture in the

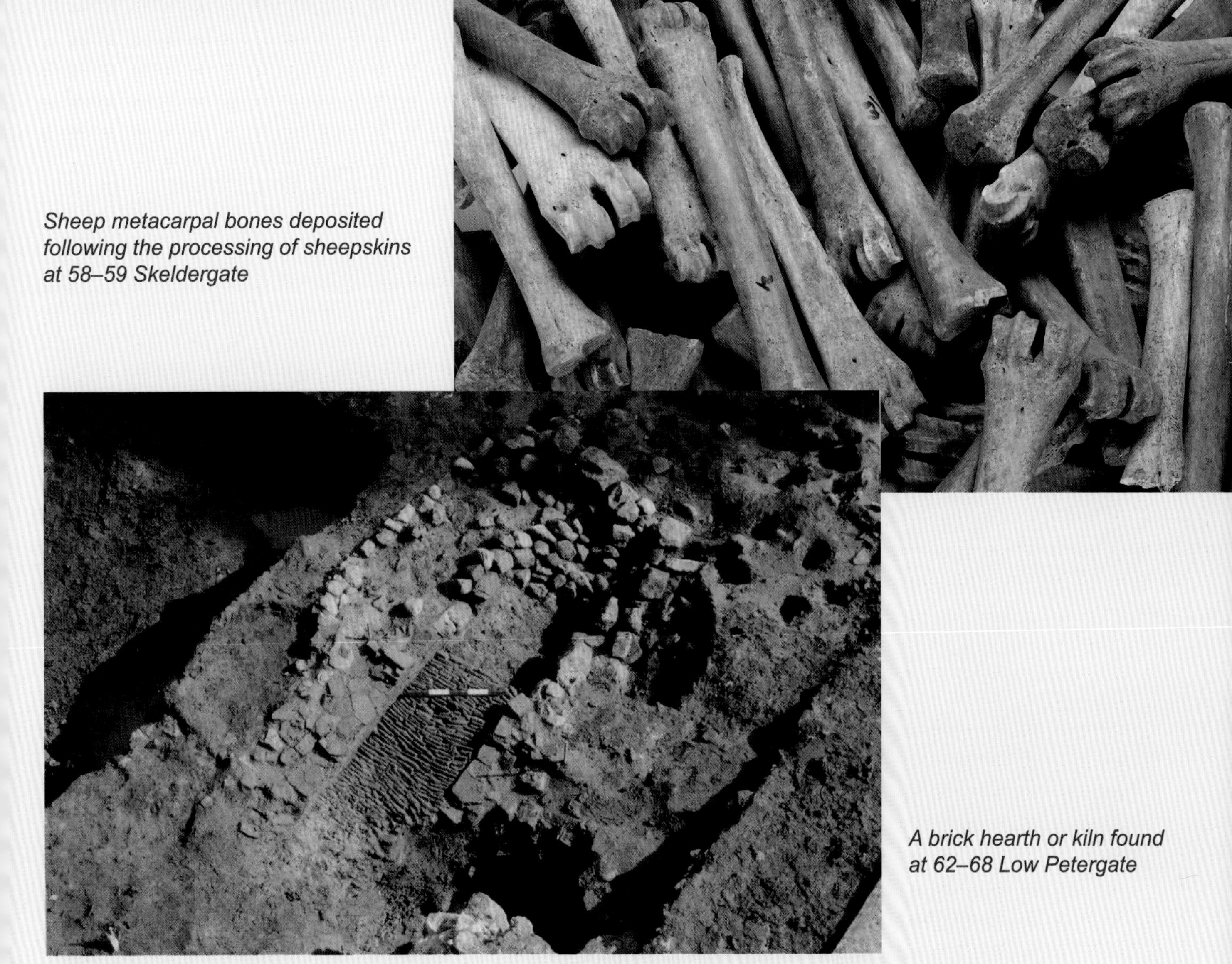

Sheep metacarpal bones deposited following the processing of sheepskins at 58–59 Skeldergate

A brick hearth or kiln found at 62–68 Low Petergate

14th century. Evidence of contemporary pin-making, also utilising copper-alloy wire, was found on the same site, with further evidence being found in excavations nearby on Hungate in 2005–2011.

A possible glaziers workshop at the rear of Blake Street and Stonegate was identified by the recovery of over 2,500 window glass fragments in a late 15th–early 16th century pit. Although the glaziers do not appear to have participated in their own pageant according to the late 15th century Register, they certainly had their own guild in York, and worshipped at the church of St Helen's at the end of Stonegate.

At 16–22 Coppergate, the retrieval of at least 18 bale pins has been interpreted as pointing to the presence on the site of a woolpacker in the medieval period; a significantly larger number found in excavations on Carmelite Street in 1991 may also suggest the transport of wool bales via the site in the late medieval period.

Guildhalls

Guildhalls were built as meeting places for guild members, where they could conduct business, and discuss their social and religious obligations. In the 14th century it was common for the crafts to hold their meetings in the churches with which they were associated: for example, the weavers met in All Saints church, North Street, and the pinners and butchers in St Crux near The Shambles. Others used rooms in the houses of religious orders, including the cordwainers who met in the Carmelite Friary in Hungate. Later in the 14th century, some guilds built their own guildhalls, but these were a minority, and most continued to meet in churches.

Stone corbel found in the Hungate excavations. Originally from a church, it was re-used in the foundations of the Cordwainers' Hall

The sole surviving craft guildhall in York is that of the Merchant Taylors (Tailors) in Aldwark, but records indicate that both the butchers' and cordwainers' guilds had their own halls at certain periods. These no longer exist, but archaeological excavations at Hungate have revealed physical evidence of the cordwainers' guildhall. Other surviving guildhalls are that of the trading company The Merchant Adventurers on Fossgate, and the hall of the religious guild of St Anthony/ St Martin at St Anthony's Hall, Peasholme Green.

Entrance to the Merchant Adventurers' Hall on Fossgate

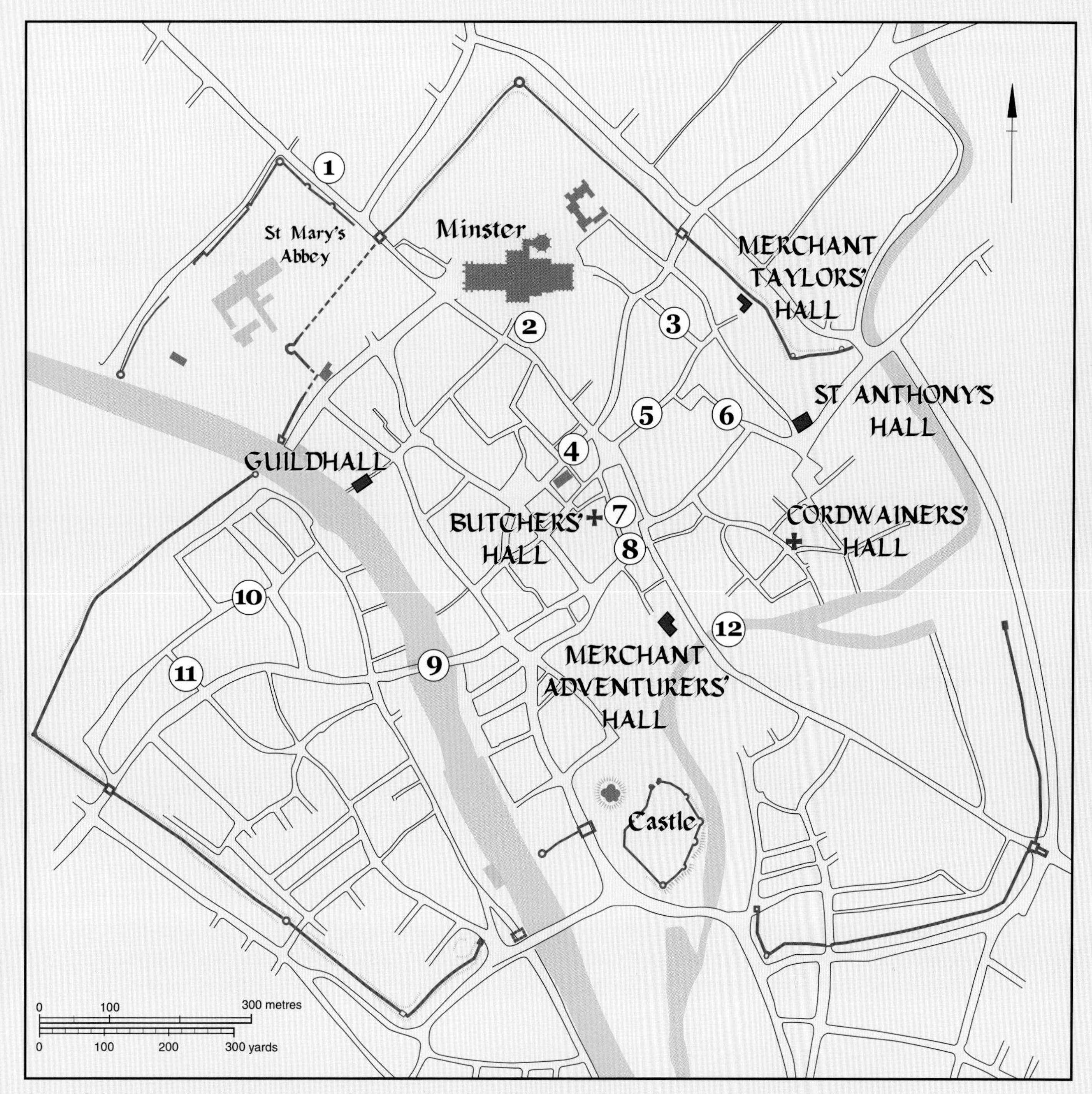

Map of York showing the locations of the medieval guild halls and streets associated with the guilds

1. *Bootham (Cutlers)*
2. *Minster Gates (Goldsmiths)*
3. *Bedern (Founders)*
4. *Church Street (Girdlers)*
5. *St Andrewgate (Smiths)*
6. *Spen Lane (Smiths)*
7. *The Shambles (Butchers)*
8. *St Crux (Pinners)*
9. *Ouse Bridge (Fishers)*
10. *Tanner Row (Barkers)*
11. *Barker Lane (Barkers)*
12. *Foss Bridge (Fishers)*

The Merchant Taylors' Hall, Aldwark

Craft guildhalls

The Merchant Taylors' Guildhall

In the medieval period, the tailors were closely associated with the religious and charitable confraternity of St John the Baptist, and it was that fraternity which built the hall: a document of c.1415 refers to it as 'the land and hall of the fraternity of St John the Baptist'. The large hall was probably built in the late 14th century, with the smaller wing added later. Originally half-timbered, the building was encased in brick in the late 17th–early 18th century. A small excavation in 1991 exposed a complex series of buildings adjacent to the hall. The earliest remains exposed consisted of a tile hearth and robbed limestone wall, perhaps part of an earlier hall for the St John the Baptist Guild.

The Butchers' Guildhall

The butchers' guildhall lay behind The Shambles in Gell Garth, an area owned by the guild until 1929, and now occupied by York market. At the same time, the butchers maintained a chapel in the nearby church of St Crux.

The Cordwainers' Guildhall

The location of the cordwainers' guildhall on Hungate is clearly linked to their tradition of meeting in the Carmelite Friary in the same area. In the 16th century the cordwainers appear to have purchased land after the demolition and sale of the church and churchyard of St John the Baptist. During excavations at Hungate, part of a stone building thought to have been the cordwainers' hall was identified on the corner of Hungate and Pound Lane; it was found to have been constructed on top of burials and it incorporated re-used limestone blocks, including an ecclesiastical limestone corbel, into its foundations. It was probably demolished c.1810.

Other guildhalls

The Merchant Adventurers' Hall

In a similar way to the Merchant Taylors, The Company of Merchant Adventurers had its origins in a religious guild, which was dedicated to Our Lord Jesus Christ and the Blessed Virgin Mary. The members of that guild built the Hall in Fossgate in the 14th century; by 1430 most members were mercers, who set up a trading guild alongside the fraternity. Mercers were originally the sellers of cloth, mostly imported, but later they sold all sorts of imported goods.

The Merchant Adventurers' Hall, Fossgate

St Anthony's Hall, Peasholme Green

Initially there were just three rooms in the building, with the main hall on the upper floor, a hospital in the undercroft, and a chapel, the last being rebuilt around 1411. In the later 16th century a north wing was added, and the entrance building was constructed or rebuilt.

In 1995, trial excavations within the undercroft revealed that the original floor lies relatively close to the present surface. Well-preserved evidence for a series of alterations to the internal layout of the building also survived, including a series of brick alignments, interpreted as the bases for partitions which subdivided the hospital in the undercroft. Amongst the finds from this excavation was a magnificent 14th-century gold brooch with the inscription IH SUS NAZ (Jesus of Nazareth) (*see p.44*).

St Anthony's Hall

The religious guild of St Anthony, also known as the guild of St Martin, had its origins in the 15th century. Its hall with chapel was built by the guild in about 1450, with the larger eastern part of the building added between c.1485 and 1500. After the Dissolution, it was taken on by the city authorities, who allowed trade guilds with no hall of their own to use it for meetings.

York City Guildhall or Common Hall

The Guildhall is first mentioned in 1256, but the existing building dates to 1445, when the city corporation and St Christopher's guild agreed to share the expenses of a new hall. It seems to have taken some years for building to be completed, with the first record of a council meeting being held there in May 1459. The whole site was taken over by the city in 1549, and council meetings are still held in the building.

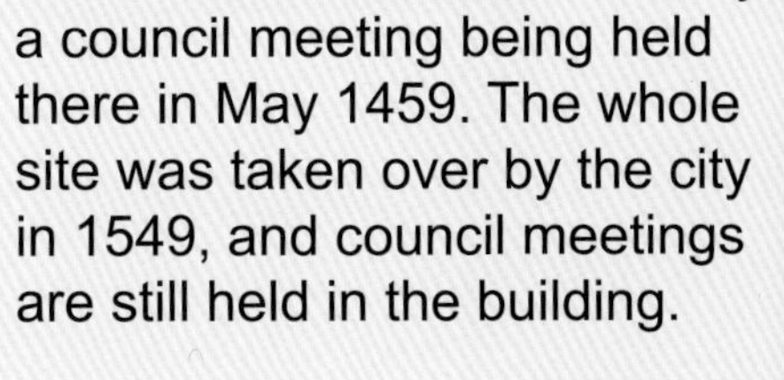

Interior of York City Guildhall

The Guildhall from the river

The Nativity *and (below)* The Crucifixion, *from the 2002 and 2010 wagon productions of the Mystery Plays*

The Corpus Christi Play

In an age when most people could not read, and the Bible was written in Latin, the individual pageants which made up the Corpus Christi play were designed to give the city's inhabitants instruction in their Christian faith in an accessible and entertaining way. The plays were not only written in a language that all could understand, but they were performed by the citizens themselves, and many in the audience would have recognised actors taking part as family members, friends or workmates. Apart from a few exceptions, the plays are believed to have been acted out on an annual basis until the late 16th century. The miraculous survival of a manuscript of the text of all the plays, written some time between 1463 and 1477 on 268 pages of parchment and bound between wooden boards covered in leather, has enabled the same plays to be brought to life in modern times. Since their first revival in 1951, the plays have been regularly performed, both as static productions at St Mary's Abbey, the Theatre Royal and in York Minster, and – more authentically – on wagons moving around the city, just as they would have been seen in the Middle Ages.

York Guild of Building presents The Creation *in the revived wagon plays, seen here in Deans Park in 2010*

First performances

The feast of Corpus Christi is first known to have been celebrated in York Minster in 1325, and included the carrying of the consecrated host in processions, one of which took place within the city and was organised by the city authorities. The craft guilds took part in this procession, and by 1376 it is clear that pageants were associated with the feast day. Occasional disputes flared up between some of the guilds, perhaps to do with the designated order in which they processed, and some felt that the drinking and carousing which took place around the pageants were not appropriate in a religious celebration. So in 1426 it was decided that the pageants and the procession should occur on consecutive days, with the procession being held on the day following Corpus Christi Day. The idea of the procession helps to explain the tradition of performing the pageants on wagons which took a pre-ordained route around the city. The connection between the performances and the celebration of the Corpus Christi feast may also have been a practical one, in that the entire cycle has been estimated to take approximately 20 hours to complete; performing in mid-summer would take advantage of the longest hours of daylight of the year, the first pageant being expected to start at 4.30–5am, as dawn was breaking.

Noah's Ark presented as a wagon play in Minster Yard, 2002

The earliest detailed account of the pageants dates to 1415, in the form of the 'Ordo Paginarum' or 'Order of the Pageants', which lists the guilds, the pageant each performed, and the order in which they were presented, but it is clear that there were some alterations to this order over succeeding years. The surviving texts, in the form of the 'Register' of the Corpus Christi play, date to sometime between 1463 and 1477, and the list associated with the Register differs from that of 50 years earlier, with some pageants revised, and some reassigned to different guilds. This manuscript of the Register was the city's official record of the cycle, and it was compiled from the textual copies, held by the guilds, of the individual pageants; only one original guild text (the scriveners' *The Incredulity of Thomas*) now survives. The Register would be checked against the performances; for example, in 1554 John Clerke recorded that the girdlers' pageant was so altered that it no longer matched his version, a clear indication that the plays developed over the years.

The assignment of the plays to the guilds was not always carried out arbitrarily, some pageants having obvious links to the guilds which performed them. Some of these links would have been more apparent to the medieval audiences than they might be to us; for example, the subject matter of a pageant may relate to the saint or biblical event supported by the guild. This was the case with the carpenters, who performed *The Resurrection*; their guild was also known as the Holy Fraternity of the Resurrection. Other links were made with the trade and/or tools used by the guilds; a clear instance of this is the bakers, who performed *The Last Supper*, where bread was a significant element in the play.

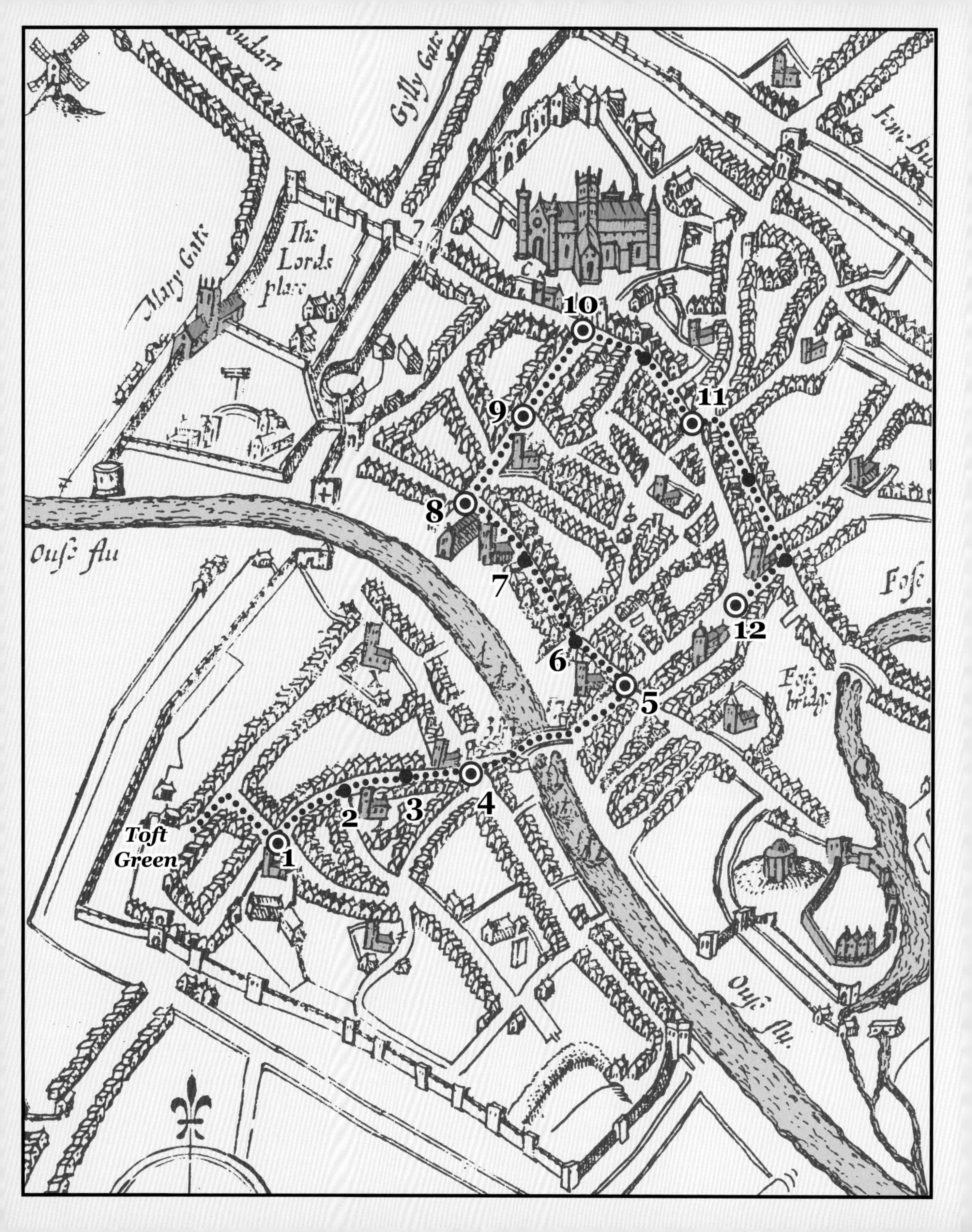

Toft Green
1
2
3
4
5
6
7
8
9
10
11
12
The Lords place
Mary Gate
Gylly Gate
Ouse flu

Preparations for the pageants

Early in Lent, the city authorities would formally instruct the guilds to bring forth their pageants on Corpus Christi Day. Each guild had a pageant master, whose first task was to collect the 'pageant silver' from guild members in order to cover expenses; these would include the storage and maintenance of the pageant wagon, and the purchase and repairing of props and costumes, as well as the provision of refreshments for the actors during rehearsals and performances.

The wooden wagon provided the stage, and it would be custom-designed for each pageant. It would probably have at least two levels, the lower part being shrouded all round to provide an area for the performers to hide in when not on stage, and also for any equipment needed for the stage effects. The upper level was open to the air, and the whole wagon was strung with banners. It might feature lifting gear and moving scenery. When not in use, the pageant wagons were kept in pageant houses or sheds at Pageant Green (now Toft Green), which also marked the assembly point for all the wagons on the day. Typically there would be 12 stations (as in the 12 stations of the Cross), points at which each performance would be undertaken, and each provided with a scaffold for wealthier members of the audience to be seated (at a charge), and a processional route banner. The route itself never varied (see map), but the positions of the stations were let to the highest bidder, and some might be altered from year to year. The first station, however, was always at the gates of the Benedictine Priory of the Holy Trinity on Micklegate – part of the church of the priory survives in the nave of the present Holy Trinity church. Here the civic clerk would sit and check the plays against his register. Station number 8 was close to the Guildhall, which was where members of the city corporation could watch the performances, and number 10 was at the Minster Gates. The final station was at Pavement, in the heart of the city. It must have been a great task to ensure that all the wagons, which were pulled by men rather than animals, proceeded in a timely fashion, so that the whole Corpus Christi play did not overrun. The threat of fines being imposed on a guild if its pageant hindered an orderly run must have helped to keep things moving smoothly.

Facing page: Map of the Route of the Mystery Plays
(map after John Speed, 1610)

Station 1: Holy Trinity Priory, Micklegate
Stations 2 and 3: Further down Micklegate
Station 4: Skeldergate/North Street junction
Station 5: Church of St Michael the Archangel (Spurriergate)
Stations 6 and 7: Further down Spurriergate, onto Coney Street
Station 8: City Guildhall
Station 9: Stonegate
Station 10: Minster Gates
Station 11: King's Square
Station 12: All Saints, Pavement

The performances

There are few clues in the surviving documents about visual aspects of the performances; stage directions are scarce and it is not always clear how different locations within the same pageant were portrayed. In some instances, the wagon would have represented one location, and the street itself another. By being so close to the action, the audience could feel more involved, rather than being mere bystanders; no doubt, they also recognised friends and neighbours in the performances. Some people may not have been readily identifiable, however, as masks were regularly used, particularly by characters such as angels and devils, while God may have worn a gilded visor. Wigs and beards would have been needed, the former particularly in the case of the female characters, all of whom would have been played by men. Clothing would have been of contemporary style, with those of higher rank, such as the Magi, wearing regal costume, whilst the biblical soldiers and peasants may well have been dressed in clothes very familiar to those watching them perform. Finally, music would have played an important role in the productions. In most cases, this would be singing rather than purely instrumental music, often covering action where there was no accompanying dialogue, and perhaps most notably featuring in scenes where God appears, as an essential feature in the depiction of heaven.

The audience experience of the pageants is not recorded, and it is not known how many would have watched the performances. Some craft members were ordered to attend the play put on by their own guild from first to last performance, with a fine to be paid for any absence. Some stations may have afforded better views than others, but it is quite likely that the audience members would have moved around during the long day, perhaps missing one episode in order to eat or meet friends, only to catch it up elsewhere. It would surely have been a very different experience to that of watching a static theatre performance, and arguably a more intimate and involving one.

List of the Pageants

A complete list of the pageants in the York Cycle, probably dating to c.1450–75.

Bold type indicates discussion of that guild in the text.

1. **The Barkers (tanners): *The Fall of the Angels***
2. The Plasterers: *The Creation*
3. The Cardmakers (makers of wool-carding combs): *The Creation of Adam and Eve*
4. The Fullers (cloth-finishers): *Adam and Eve in Eden*
5. **The Coopers (barrel-makers): *The Fall of Man***
6. **The Armourers: *The Expulsion***
7. The Glovers: *Cain and Abel*
8. **The Shipwrights: *The Building of the Ark***
9. **The Fishers and Mariners: *The Flood***
10. The Parchmentmakers and Bookbinders: *Abraham and Isaac*
11. The Hosiers (makers of hose): *Moses and Pharaoh*
12. The Spicers: *The Annunciation and Visitation*
13. **The Pewterers and Founders: *Joseph's Trouble about Mary***
14. **The Tile Thatchers: *The Nativity***
15. The Chandlers (candle-makers): *The Shepherds*
16. **The Masons and Goldsmiths: *Herod and the Magi***
17. St Leonard's Hospital: *The Purification*
18. **The Marshals (farriers): *The Flight into Egypt***
19. **The Girdlers and Nailers: *The Slaughter of the Innocents***
20. **The Spurriers and Lorimers: *Christ with the Doctors in the Temple***
21. The Barbers: *The Baptism*
22. **The Smiths: *The Temptation***
23. The Vintners: *The Marriage at Cana*
24. **The Curriers: *The Transfiguration***
25. The Ironmongers: *Jesus in the House of Simon the Leper*
26. The Cappers (cap-makers): *The Woman Taken in Adultery/The Raising of Lazarus*
27. The Skinners: *The Entry into Jerusalem*
28. **The Cutlers: *The Conspiracy***
29. The Baxters (bakers): *The Last Supper*
30. **The Cordwainers (shoe-makers): *The Agony in the Garden and the Betrayal***
31. The Bowyers and Fletchers (makers of bows and arrows): *Christ Before Annas and Caiaphas*
32. The Tapiters and Couchers (makers of worsted cloth and bed hangings): *Christ before Pilate I/The Dream of Pilate's Wife*
33. The Liststers (dyers): *Christ Before Herod*
34. **The Cooks and Waterleaders (water-sellers): *The Remorse of Judas***
35. The Tilemakers: *Christ Before Pilate 2/The Judgement*
36. The Shearmen (cloth-finishers): *The Road to Calvary*
37. **The Pinners: *The Crucifixion***
38. **The Butchers: *The Death of Christ***
39. The Saddlers: *The Harrowing of Hell*
40. **The Carpenters: *The Resurrection***
41. The Winedrawers (wine-makers): *Christ's Appearance to Mary Magdalen*
42. **The Woolpackers: *The Supper at Emmaus***
43. **The Scriveners (writers): *The Incredulity of Thomas***
44. **The Tailors: *The Ascension***
45. The Potters: *Pentecost*
46. The Drapers: *The Death of the Virgin*
47. The Linenweavers: *The Funeral of the Virgin*
48. The Woollenweavers: *The Assumption of the Virgin*
49. The Hostelers (innkeepers): *The Coronation of the Virgin*
50. The Mercers (merchants): *The Last Judgement*

Taken from Beadle and King 1984 (reissued 2009)

The Guild of the

BARKERS

The barkers, also known as tanners, undertook the tanning of cow and ox hides, the first stage in making leather. The aim of tanning was to remove water from the hide. The first job was to remove the horns and hooves, then the hair and fat needed to be scraped off, and the hides soaked in a series of liquors, usually made with oak bark (hence barkers). These liquors were at first mild, but were gradually increased in strength, and the hides could be left to soak in them for nine months or more; the longer the process took, the better the quality of the leather. Finally the leather had to be properly dried. Leather that had been simply tanned was called red leather because of the colour, but at this stage it was still unsuitable for working; it then needed to be passed to the curriers for the next stage in the process, after which the leather was described as black.

Bark rolls collected for supply to the tanning industry (16–22 Coppergate)

The amount of water required to tan hides meant that tanning tended to be carried out close to rivers, and evidence from place-names and written records shows that this was the case in York. Tanner Row was originally known as Barker Row, which is first recorded as a street name in the 16th century, and poll tax returns of 1381 record that 41 of 43

tanners listed lived in the parish of All Saints North Street in which Tanner Row is situated; the Orders of Angels window in the church of All Saints North Street includes an image of a tanner with his tools.

Several tanners' wills survive from the 15th and 16th centuries, indicating that they were resident in parishes along Walmgate, and were thus presumably using the Foss as their water source.

The Barkers' Pageant:
The Fall of the Angels
(Pageant 1 of 50)

The play depicts the first moments of the creation of the earth, and of the angels. The disobedient Lucifer boasts of his power, and is suddenly cast down with other rebellious angels and devils into hell. God continues with his creation, providing light where there had originally been darkness.

As members of the hugely important leather industry which employed a large number of workers throughout the medieval period, the barkers had ownership of the first pageant in the cycle, a position which surely reflected the prestige of their guild. The performance began at 4.30am, resulting in the dramatic effect of the rising of the sun coinciding with the presentation of the themes of the creation and of light (the literal meaning of Lucifer being 'light bearing'). No doubt the filthy nature of the tanning process with its pits of noxious substances was recognised by the audience as being reflected in the pit of filth (hell) into which Lucifer falls, making this a particularly appropriate pageant for the barkers.

The Guild of the

COOPERS

Coopers made stave-built wooden vessels, mainly buckets, tubs, and casks, constructed using narrow staves of wood bound together by wooden or metal bands. Watertight casks were used to contain fermented liquids such as ale, and these often had bowed sides and vent holes. Oak was particularly favoured for these casks as it is hardwearing and impervious to liquid. Dry goods such as wheat, fish or soap did not usually need to be in watertight containers. Casks were used for storage and for the transportation of commercial goods; they were often re-used as linings for wells and latrines, some of which were deep enough to require three tiers of casks. Tubs were often made from cut-down casks, but were not sealed with lids.

The bucket as found in a barrel well

Wooden bucket with iron bands (16–22 Coppergate)

The middle cask of a three-tier cask or barrel well (Bedern Foundry)

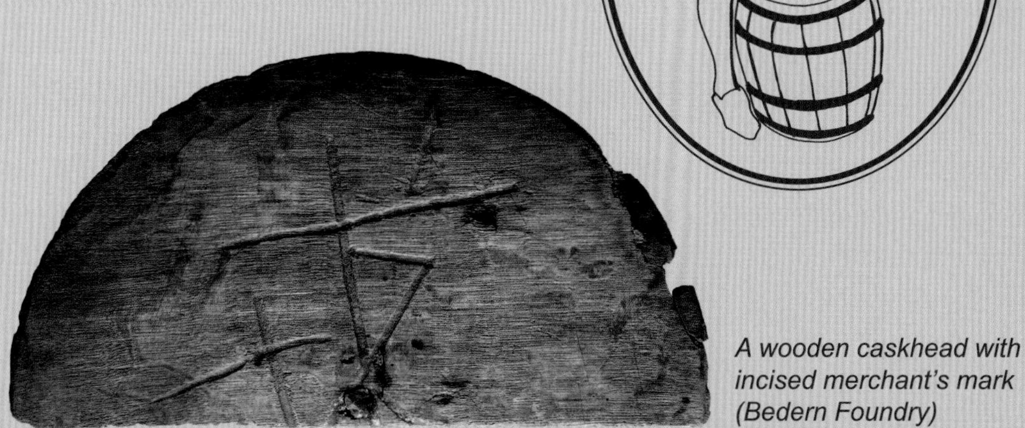

A wooden caskhead with incised merchant's mark (Bedern Foundry)

Coopering was a skilled trade, the necessary skills having to be taught and acquired by experience. Coopers needed not only to know how to make the vessels, but also that there were rules about the capacities of casks, which were laid down by the guild, which assigned particular names to different sizes of cask. Ale and beer, for example, were stored in barrels, a barrel being one specific size; other recorded names included kilderkins (half barrels) and firkins.

The Coopers' Pageant:
The Fall of Man

(Pageant 5 of 50)

Satan returns full of envy for mankind because he knows that God intends to take man's form. He turns into a snake and using flattery, seduction and bullying, persuades Eve to eat the apple; she in turn offers it to Adam. They are banished by God from the Garden of Eden.

The Guild of the

ARMOURERS

Armourers in medieval York seem mainly to have produced swords, comprising iron blades, and hilts and guards of metal or organic materials, but they also made leather scabbards. This is clear from their ordinances of 1475, which required that they ‘dight no swerds but workmanlyke’ and make no ‘skabberds but of good stuf’. Plate armour itself was often imported, for example from London, where complaints were made by residents in 1377 about one armourer, as a result of ‘the blows of the sledge-hammers when the great pieces of iron called “Osmond” are being wrought … and the stench of the smoke from the sea-coal used in the forge [which] penetrates their hall and chambers’. Although they did not make plate armour, York’s armourers could refurbish it, but they were specifically forbidden to tout for work by harassing knights and gentlemen to have their armour smartened up.

A leather sword scabbard which has subsequently been cut down (12–18 Swinegate)

Armourers might also be required to make chain mail from iron wire for the more lowly soldiers who were unable to afford plate armour. Mail-making was sometimes considered fiddly work, and might be carried out by women.

Copper alloy finger-joint covers, possibly from the same pair of plate armour gauntlets (16–22 Coppergate)

Iron chain mail – one set of mail has become corroded onto a pot sherd (1–9 Bridge Street)

The Armourers' Pageant:
Expulsion from Eden
(Pageant 6 of 50)

In this pageant, God's condemnation of Adam and Eve is repeated by the angel of their banishment, whilst Adam and Eve reproach each other and make excuses. Eventually both are regretful but resigned, and Adam prays to God for His help.

The Guild of the

SHIPWRIGHTS

It seems most likely that shipwrights in medieval York would primarily have repaired boats rather than building them, but written accounts exist for the construction of a royal galley, barge and 'navicula' (small ship) in York during the 1290s, so the construction of new vessels clearly did occur. It is not known where these particular vessels were constructed, but in the later 14th century, boat-building is recorded as taking place in what is now St George's Field.

With constant river traffic travelling up and down the Ouse, there would certainly have been plenty of custom for the repair of boats. These would have been clinker-built vessels in the main, constructed using overlapping timbers, held in place with iron clench bolts, and caulked or waterproofed with tarred animal fibres.

When it became impossible to repair a vessel, it would often be broken up and the timbers re-used. At Coppergate, a wooden revetment at the edge of the River Foss was found to have been made using old boat timbers; the three largest fragments of clinker-boat boards, with clench bolts in situ, were all so similar that they were thought to derive from the same vessel. Traces of closely spaced wooden trenails that originally fastened the framing timbers were also found, suggesting that the vessel from which the timbers originated was probably a trading craft. Each of the boards had been much patched, suggesting that when broken up for re-use the vessel had been so old and worn as to be no longer suitable for use on the water. An approximate date for the boat was provided by tree ring analysis; the wood was identified as Baltic oak which had been felled at some time after 1376. It was not possible to determine whether the boat itself, or the timbers, had been imported, but the latter was thought more likely.

Iron clench bolts (16–22 Coppergate)

A boat timber with caulking and clench bolts (Coppergate Watching Brief)

The Shipwrights' Pageant:
The Building of the Ark
(Pageant 8 of 50)

God instructs Noah to build the ark, despite Noah's protests that he does not know how to make a ship. Noah then describes how he makes the ship, which must be clinker-built, as he notes the use of clench nails. Finally, God tells Noah to collect together the animals and his family so that they may be saved from the flood.

Unlike other Mystery Play cycles, York was unique in dividing the story of Noah into two separate episodes, the Building of the Ark and the Flood. The detailing of the Ark's construction with its use of technical vocabulary enabled a demonstration of the shipwrights' skills in the pageant; indeed it seems that a representation of the vessel took shape in front of the audience. Noah's monologue describes his actions, cutting the boards to the correct thickness, securing the joins with clamps, sealing the joints, and fixing the clench nails. The audience would have been left in no doubt that great skill was required to build a ship.

The Guild of the

FISHERS and MARINERS

Fish bones of cod, herring and eel, marine species all found in medieval York

Fish represented a very significant element of the medieval diet; the consumption of meat was banned by the Church on religious grounds during Lent and on Fridays, days on which fish could be consumed instead.

York records note numerous 'Fishers' who provided freshwater fish to be sold at market at the east end of Ouse Bridge. Much of the freshwater fish sold in York was caught in fishgarths, timber and wicker structures strung across the river. A survey of 1484 listed 44 fishgarths on the Ouse, of which three-quarters were owned by ecclesiastical institutions which rented them out to the fishers. Some of this fish may have been collected and processed at Fishergate, which had been so named by the late 11th century.

Archaeological evidence provided by fish bones indicates that while freshwater fish such as eel and carp were particularly exploited in the Anglian and Anglo-Scandinavian periods in York, marine fish – notably herring – became more important in the medieval period, although freshwater fish (typically smaller than those found in earlier periods) were also still being eaten. This change in supply may have been the result of overfishing of freshwater fish, probably combined with a rising population. This impacted on the fishmongers, for they traded primarily in freshwater fish, the trade in marine fish being dominated by merchants who sold them from Foss Bridge.

The mariners – who joined with the fishers to put on the pageant – were the men who handled river traffic between Hull and York and along the Upper Ouse.

Lead-alloy net weights used in either river or sea fishing (16–22 Coppergate; 46–54 Fishergate)

Iron fish hooks – both with and without barbs – were used (16–22 Coppergate)

Fishers' and Mariners' Pageant:
The Flood
(Pageant 9 of 50)

Noah and his family get onto the ark, although Noah's wife refuses for some time to go. The animals are cared for, and finally they see signs of land. Noah sends the dove which returns with the olive branch, and the family rejoices.

The appropriateness of this play to the fishers and mariners is quite obvious, and it is dramatically referenced in particular by Noah taking soundings of the water to determine the depth of the flood. This action was one that had to be taken constantly in coastal and river sailing, and clearly demonstrated the association of the crafts of the mariners and fishers with the story of Noah.

The Guild of the

PEWTERERS and FOUNDERS

The pewterers and the founders both made objects of non-ferrous metals. The pewterers made pewter items, particularly tableware, but they also cast dress accessories such as badges and belt decorations. Prior to c.1300, pewter had been exclusively used for church plate, but during the first half of the 14th century, domestic pewter became fashionable; being much cheaper than silver, it was affordable not only by those in the higher levels of society but also by richer peasant households. From the mid-15th century onwards, the pewter industry became even more important, and by 1475, pewter was second only to cloth in importance as an export. At least one York pewterer, Thomas Snawdon, became mayor of York during this period.

A pewter chalice and paten from the burial of a 13th century priest (46–54 Fishergate)

Two fragmentary multi-piece stone moulds, used to cast decorative mounts and beads (College of the Vicars Choral, Bedern)

A tin ampulla or flask for holy oil, and a stone mould for casting an ampulla of slightly different form (Hungate; 34 Shambles)

The founders seem to have concentrated on casting small copper-alloy pots and pans for use as kitchenware, demand for which grew in the late 14th and 15th centuries. They also appear to have made dress accessories and bells. While workers in non-ferrous metals in other cities all belonged to the same craft, the York pewterers and founders were unusual in having two separate guilds; neither guild appears to have been of great size or financial means, however, as they had to join together in order to be able to put on a performance.

Decorative pewter mount (City Mills, Skeldergate)

A fragment of fired clay mould, used in the casting of a copper-alloy cauldron (Bedern Foundry)

The Pewterers' and Founders' Pageant:
Joseph's Trouble about Mary
(Pageant 13 of 50)

Joseph struggles to understand the divine mystery of the Virgin birth which is to come. He encounters the angel Gabriel who persuades him that Mary is bearing the son of God, and he returns to her, preparing to leave for Bethlehem.

The pageant uses two locations for the action: the wilderness where Joseph meets the angel, and Mary's dwelling. It seems likely that, in the latter, metal domestic utensils made by the members of the two crafts could have featured as props.

The Guild of the TILERS or TILETHATCHERS

The tilers, or tile thatchers, were roofers, called ‘thatchers’ because the roof tiles that they used were known as ‘thaktiles’. They put up roofs using tiles supplied to them by tile-makers; they also built chimneys. As brick became increasingly used in the 15th century, tilers also constructed and refashioned buildings; for example, the King’s Manor was extended and reworked in brick in the late 15th century by tiler Richard Cheryholme. As with the carpenters, most tilers were typically employed as labourers, paid by the day, and were not wealthy, generally neither making nor supplying tiles. Occasional exceptions are known, however, with a record that tiler John Sharpe sold 2400 thaktiles to the Custodians of Ouse Bridge in 1442–43.

Tilers also appear to have worked as plasterers, and vice versa, but at the time that the list of pageants was drawn up, in the third quarter of the 15th century, there appear to have been separate guilds for the two crafts, with the plasterers performing pageant 2 (*The Creation*).

Ceramic roof tiles (Hungate)

A fragment of an upright from a wooden ladder (16–22 Coppergate)

The Tile Thatchers' Pageant:
The Nativity
(Pageant 14 of 50)

Joseph and Mary are in the stable, where Mary calmly prepares to give birth and Joseph worries about the poor conditions her son will be born into. Joseph goes out to collect fuel, and when he returns, discovers that Jesus has been born.

Although one of the most important pageants in the Mystery Play cycle, the Nativity is also one of the shortest, requiring only a cast of two (Mary and Joseph) and one set. This may be one reason why the tile thatchers, one of the poorer crafts, were able to perform it. At the same time, the audience would have been able to relate the craft to this particular play – close to the start, reference is made to a hole in the roof of the ramshackle stable. Joseph notes that 'The roof is raved (torn open) above our heads'. Later on, following the birth of Christ, Joseph marvels that where it had previously been dark, now the light shines in the hole in the roof and around the Christ child.

The Guild of the

GOLDSMITHS and MASONS

Goldsmiths made jewellery and plate in gold or silver, mostly from recycled plate or coins. As silver was the basis for the country's coinage, proving the purity of these precious metals was of critical importance, and goldsmiths are amongst the earliest recorded craftsmen who formed companies to regulate their trade. Throughout much of the medieval period, York was second only to London as a major centre of goldsmiths, and by the early 15th century had its own city mark and local assay office. The Minster's demand for silver chalices and patens used in religious ceremonies – some of which also accompanied archbishops in their graves – provided a steady stream of work; there are also records of repair work being done by local goldsmiths on the shrine of St William in the Minster. It is no surprise then that the goldsmiths' workshops tended to congregate around the Minster gates.

A gold finger ring set with a natural sapphire (College of the Vicars Choral, Bedern)

A gold finger ring set with a pearl and garnets (16–22 Coppergate)

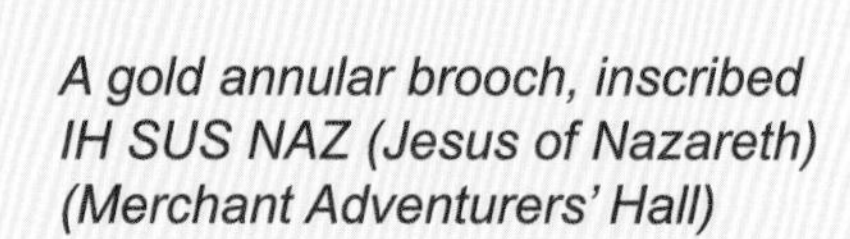

A gold annular brooch, inscribed IH SUS NAZ (Jesus of Nazareth) (Merchant Adventurers' Hall)

A length of gold wire probably for use in the making of jewellery (24–30 Tanner Row)

An annular brooch of twisted gold wire (College of the Vicars Choral, Bedern)

Some goldsmiths made considerable fortunes, and several became Lord Mayor; one of these was William Snawsell, who in the 15th century lived in what is now known as Barley Hall.

Barley Hall: the courtyard and (above) the interior of the Great Hall of the building, reconstructed to appear as it would have been in William Snawsell's time

Unlike the goldsmiths, the masons were not organised into a craft guild, mainly because their work entailed moving from job to job; this was the case even in a city like York where there was permanent work for some. Organisations based on lodges were established on large building sites, however, and the master mason of a lodge – who was also the architect responsible for the building work – would have wielded considerable power. Although not answerable to the civic authority, some of the masons nevertheless joined in with the pageants; by the later 15th century they had taken on one of the two (or even three) pageants originally brought forth by the goldsmiths.

A wooden roof boss in St Anthony's Hall showing a mason with his tools

Masons' marks and setting-out lines on a stone column base (College of the Vicars Choral, Bedern)

An iron pickaxe possibly for use by a stone mason (Bedern Foundry)

The Goldsmiths' and Masons' Pageant:
Herod and the Magi
(Pageant 16 of 50)

Herod boasts of his omnipotence to his soldiers and his son. The Three Kings meet, all having seen the star, and they agree to go to see Herod to ask his permission to pass through Jerusalem. When they advise Herod that they are travelling to see the newborn King of the Jews Herod flies into a rage, but then tells them to go and to report back to him what they find. The Kings visit Mary and praise the baby, after which an angel advises them not to return to Herod.

The staging of two pageants – *Herod* (by the masons) and *The Magi* (by the goldsmiths) – as one performance was unusual; it involved the pageant wagons and the actors of both guilds being present simultaneously at the same station, although they must have been some distance apart for the performance. While the masons presented Herod and his court on a 'Jerusalem' pageant-wagon, 'Bethlehem' and the Holy Family were offered by the goldsmiths on another. The Three Kings, provided by the goldsmiths, moved between the two wagons, possibly on horseback. The surviving manuscripts show that while there were separate texts for the two guilds, there was also a duplicate version for the part where both sets of actors were involved (when the Three Kings came to Herod's court). The suitability of the goldsmiths to take on the characters of the Magi, who no doubt carried real gold as one of their three gifts, must have been obvious to the audience.

The Guild of the

MARSHALS

Marshals were responsible for all aspects of the management and care of horses. An understanding of the work likely to have been undertaken by marshals in medieval York can be gained from the 1356 ordinances of their counterparts in London; their functions were described as including the making of horseshoes and nails and shoeing (farriery), providing advice on the purchase and cure of horses, and horse-doctoring. Treatment of sick horses involved the use of some specialist equipment, such as fleams, hand-held instruments which could relieve pressure in cases such as laminitis (inflammation of the hoof), or might be used in the lancing of inflamed gums.

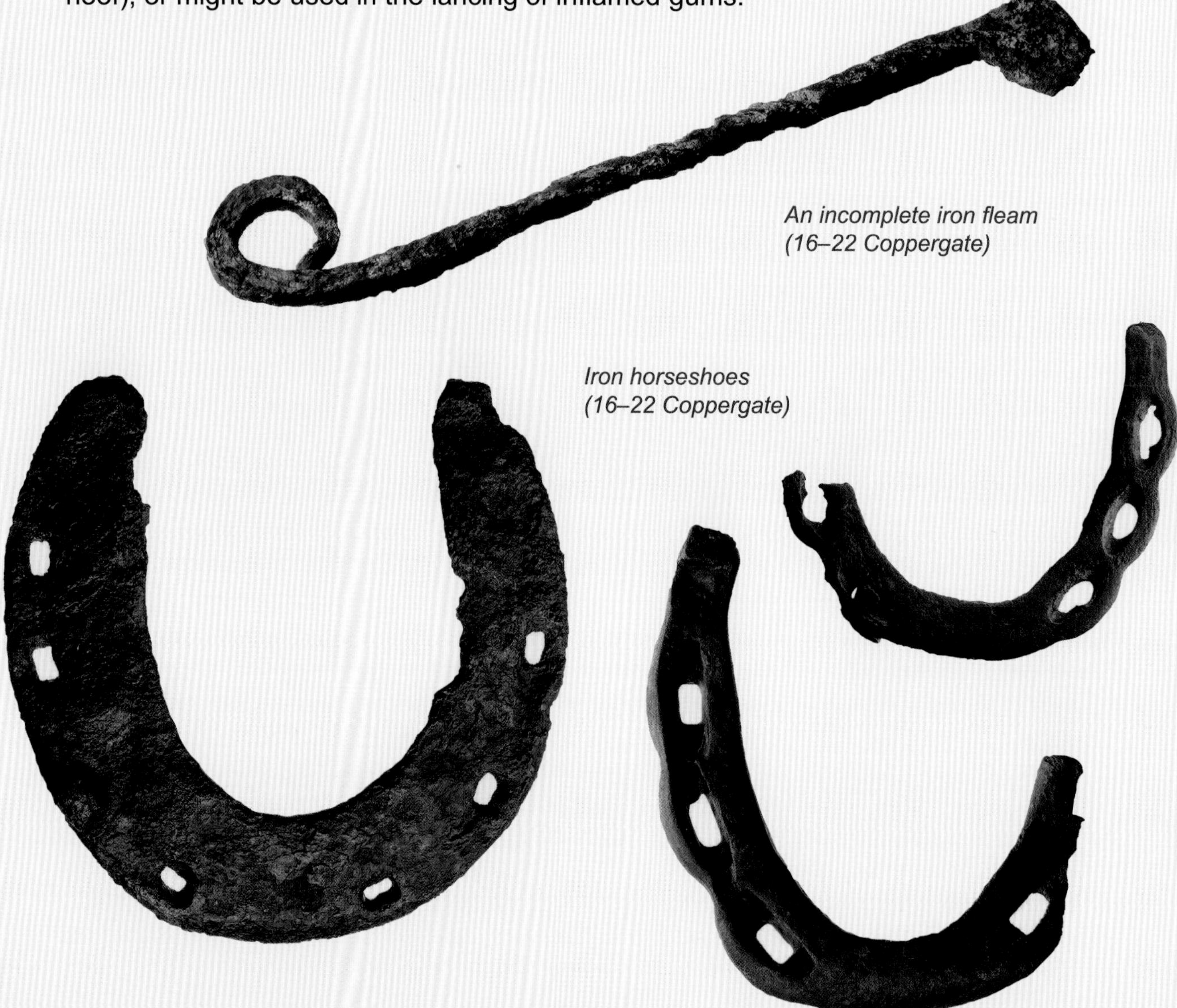

An incomplete iron fleam (16–22 Coppergate)

Iron horseshoes (16–22 Coppergate)

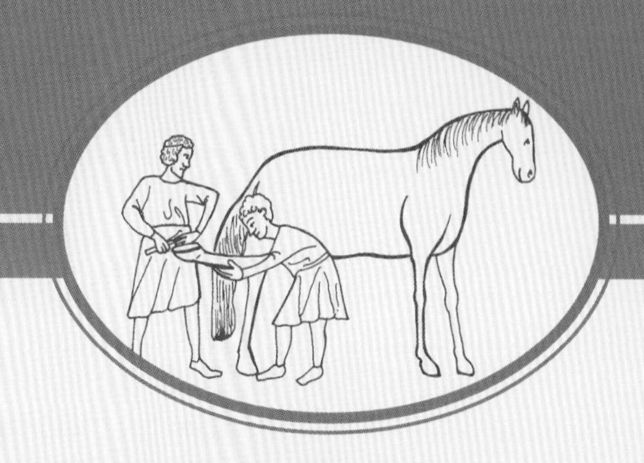

Although part of a guild that was separate from the smiths, by the 15th century both groups in York were making horseshoes and horseshoe nails which led to constant disputes, each claiming the other was stealing their legitimate work. Similar complaints by marshals about smiths were made in London, where they charged that 'many unskilled farriers were causing damage to the trade as they intermeddled with the works of farriery which they did not know how to bring to a good end, by reason whereof many horses had been lost'.

The Marshals' Pageant:
The Flight into Egypt

(Pageant 18 of 50)

Although named The Flight into Egypt, *this pageant is concerned with the Holy Family preparing to flee, as instructed by the angel Gabriel. Joseph packs up all their belongings, and they prepare to travel to Egypt, despite neither of them knowing in which direction they should go, and Mary being a poor rider. After a prayer of thanksgiving, the family rides off.*

It seems likely that a real animal would have been provided for Mary and Joseph to mount, and travel on to the next station. The marshals would, of course, have been ideally placed to supply a horse or donkey.

The Guild of the

GIRDLERS

As medieval clothing lacked pockets, belts or girdles were essential in order to carry items such as purses or knives. Recorded as important customers of the tanners and the curriers, the girdlers commonly used leather to make girdles, but they could also be made of cloth or silk. They made other leather items such as harness and dog-collars. Girdlers also seem to have manufactured metal mounts, which decorated these items, as well as buckles, ornamental fastenings, mounts, dagger chapes, purse fittings, and book clasps.

The diversity of their products led them into competition with producers and sellers of the same type of items such as smiths, tailors and lorimers, and in order to survive some diversified. It is recorded that in 1457 a girdler John Pese and his associates sold 100,000 nails to York Minster.

Part of what is now known as Church Street – which was created in 1836 – had previously been known as Girdlergate, as the result of the concentration of this craft in the district in the 14th century.

Leather girdles: one is decorated with copper-alloy bar mounts and the other with red pigment made from cinnabar (16–22 Coppergate; Bedern Foundry)

Leather harness fragments with strap joins made using copper-alloy rivets with decorative mounts (Bedern Foundry)

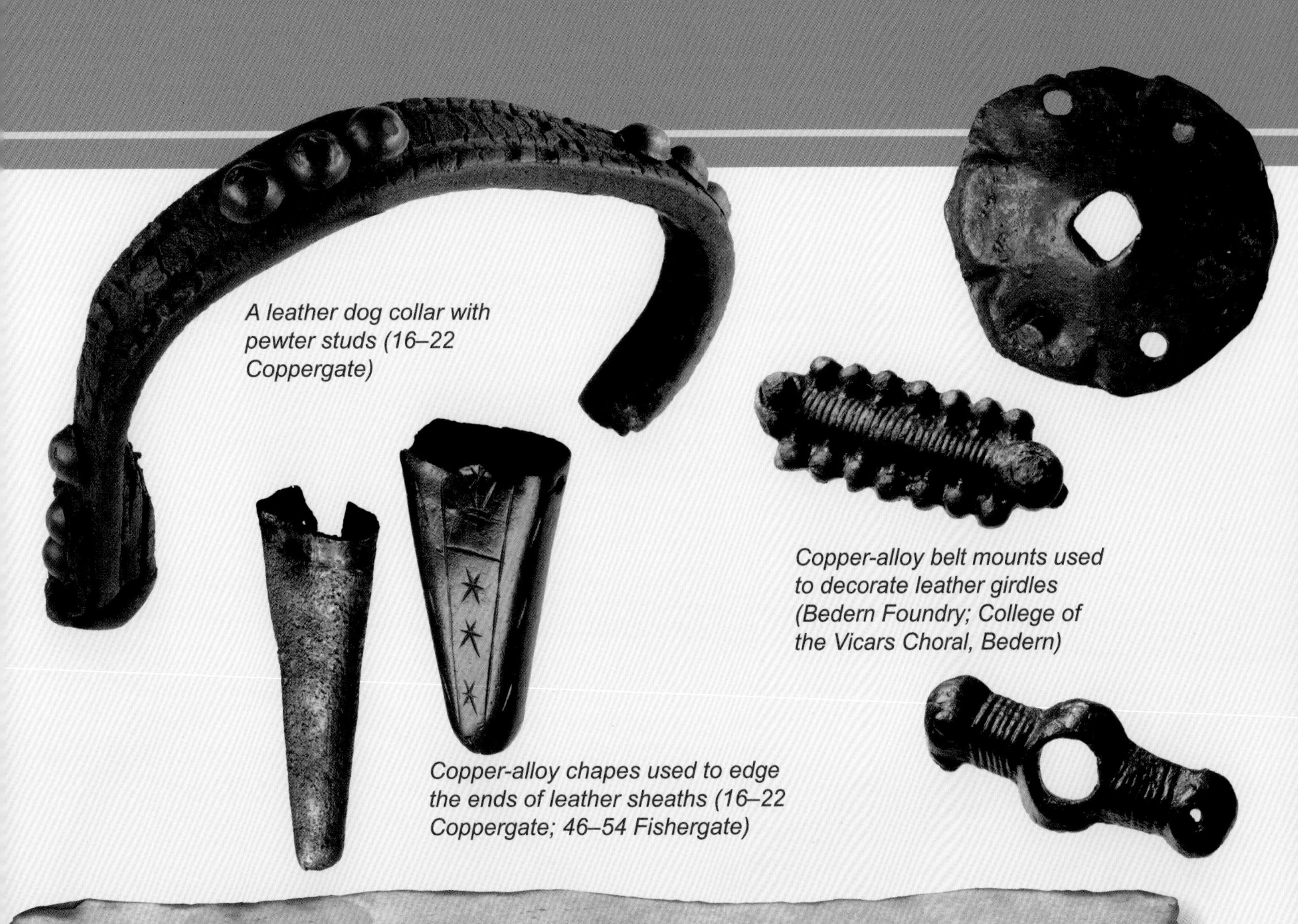

A leather dog collar with pewter studs (16–22 Coppergate)

Copper-alloy belt mounts used to decorate leather girdles (Bedern Foundry; College of the Vicars Choral, Bedern)

Copper-alloy chapes used to edge the ends of leather sheaths (16–22 Coppergate; 46–54 Fishergate)

The Girdlers' Pageant:
The Slaughter of the Innocents

(Pageant 19 of 50)

Herod hears of the birth of the newborn King of the Jews, and, upon advice from his counsellors, orders the execution of all young male children in the village of Bethlehem, so as to avoid the loss of his throne.

The conflict between the mothers and soldiers sent to carry out the massacre is movingly portrayed, and this element of the pageant was probably originally performed in the street, close to the audience. The nailers, or nail-makers, contributed to the production of this pageant in the 1470s.

The Guild of the

SPURRIERS and LORIMERS

The spurriers and lorimers tended to work together, since both crafts made metal fittings associated with horses; in the later 14th century both crafts are known to have been concentrated in the area of Spurriergate (the street of the spur-makers), Ousegate and Castlegate.

Spurs acted both functionally and as a mark of status; gilded spurs, for example, could be worn only by knights, with records suggesting that special spurs were made for jousting, although no spurs recovered have been identified as such.

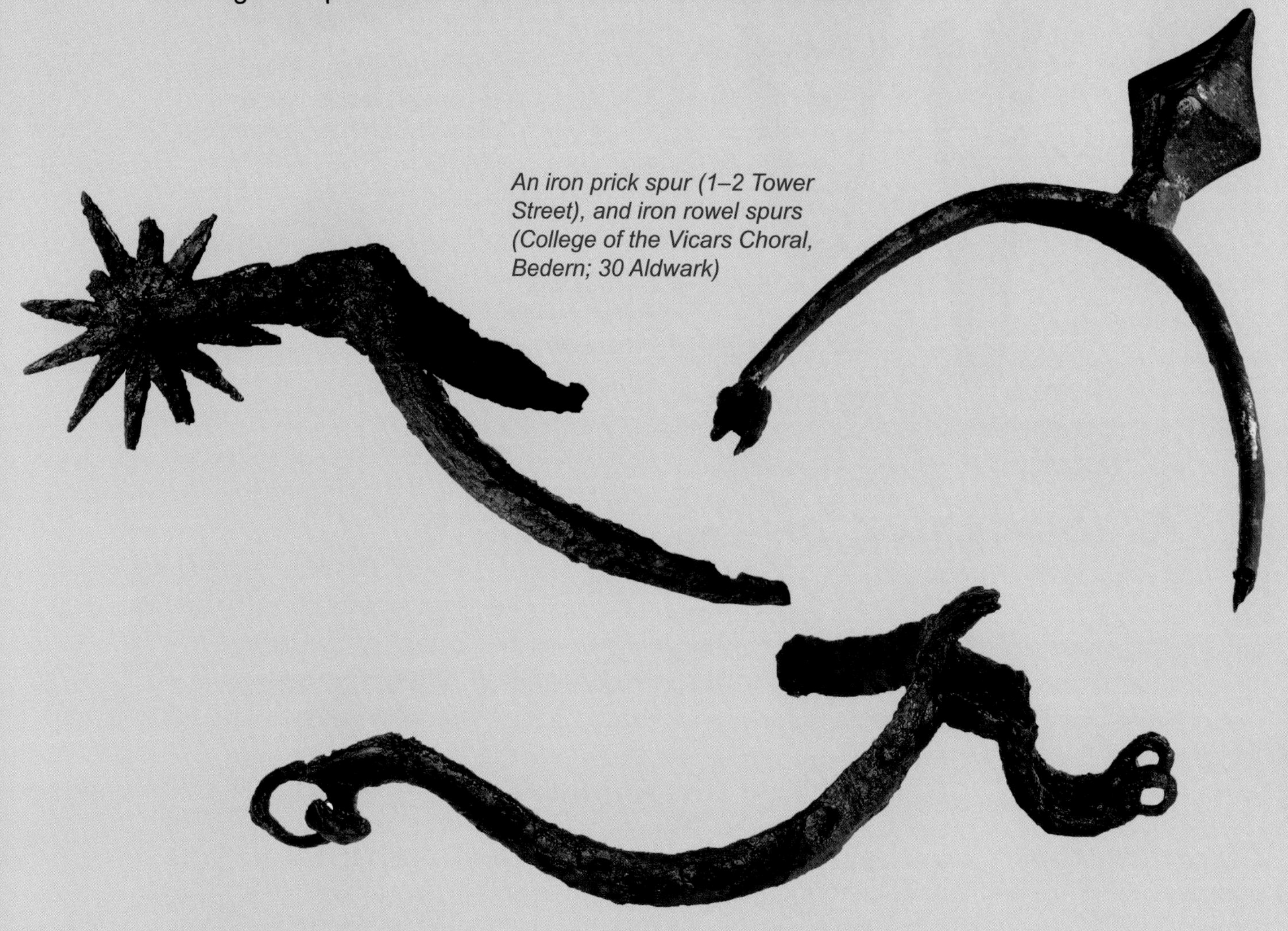

An iron prick spur (1–2 Tower Street), and iron rowel spurs (College of the Vicars Choral, Bedern; 30 Aldwark)

Lorimers made metal harness fittings such as bits and also stirrups. Unfortunately, little survives in York's medieval records about either of these crafts; in London, however, records indicate that the spurriers' reputation was at times rather poor, their working conditions leading to similar complaints to those made against the armourers. Apparently spurriers tended 'to wander about all day without working at their trade and when they are drunk and frantic, they take to their work to the annoyance of the sick and their neighbours. And then they blow up their fires so vigorously that their fires begin at once to blaze, to the great peril of themselves and the whole neighbourhood'.

An iron horse bit (16–22 Coppergate)

Spurriers' and Lorimers' Pageant:
Christ with the Doctors in the Temple
(Pageant 20 of 50)

Mary and Joseph take the 12-year-old Jesus with them to Jerusalem for the Passover. Upon discovering that he is missing, they find him in the temple, sitting with the doctors and amazing them with his knowledge.

The Guild of the

SMITHS

Smiths – or blacksmiths – worked iron, their products including structural ironwork, tools, other implements, and horseshoes. Some made more specialist items such as clocks, locks and keys. As with other hot metal activities, there were often complaints about the dirt and noise they produced, but concerns were also raised about the use of defective materials, or attempts to sell second-hand items as new. One area of particular unease was the manufacture of keys. In London, for example, blacksmiths were forbidden to make keys 'from any kind of impress thereof', but were instructed to make them from an existing key or the lock for which the key was being forged.

Iron tongs used to hold metal during working (Bedern Foundry; 46–54 Fishergate)

Iron punches used to make holes in hot metal (16–22 Coppergate; 46–54 Fishergate)

An iron pickaxe head, a tool made by a smith (62-68 Low Petergate)

A barrel padlock and padlock keys, all made of iron (16–22 Coppergate)

The Smiths' Pageant:
The Temptation
(Pageant 22 of 50)

In the first temptation Satan tempts Christ, hungry after his 40 days in the wilderness, to prove himself the Son of God by turning stones into bread. In the second temptation Satan sets Christ on the pinnacle of the Temple in Jerusalem and dares him, if he is the Son of God, to throw himself down, so that God will save him. Thirdly, the devil takes Christ to a mountain top, shows him the kingdoms of the earth, and promises them all to Christ if he will worship Satan. In all three temptations, Satan tries to make Christ misuse his powers to reveal his divine identity.

The Guild of the

CURRIERS

The curriers bought the dried red leather from the barkers and converted it into black leather, a softer and more flexible material which could then be made into shoes or other products. The process involved dampening the leather, and then softening it by pummelling or trampling; subsequently, the surfaces would be scoured with a stiff brush, and iron tools called slickers were used to remove any ingrained dirt. The flesh side would be shaved using a shaving knife with a double-edged blade until the required thickness of leather had been achieved. The shaved hides were washed clean and then worked to flatten and stretch the leather, before being impregnated with a warmed mixture of tallow (animal fat) and fish oils. Finally, the hides were dried, and any surplus grease removed; if soft leather was required, this would entail further rubbing. The leather could then be coloured or polished.

Leather shavings recovered from a late 14th century pit fill (16–22 Coppergate)

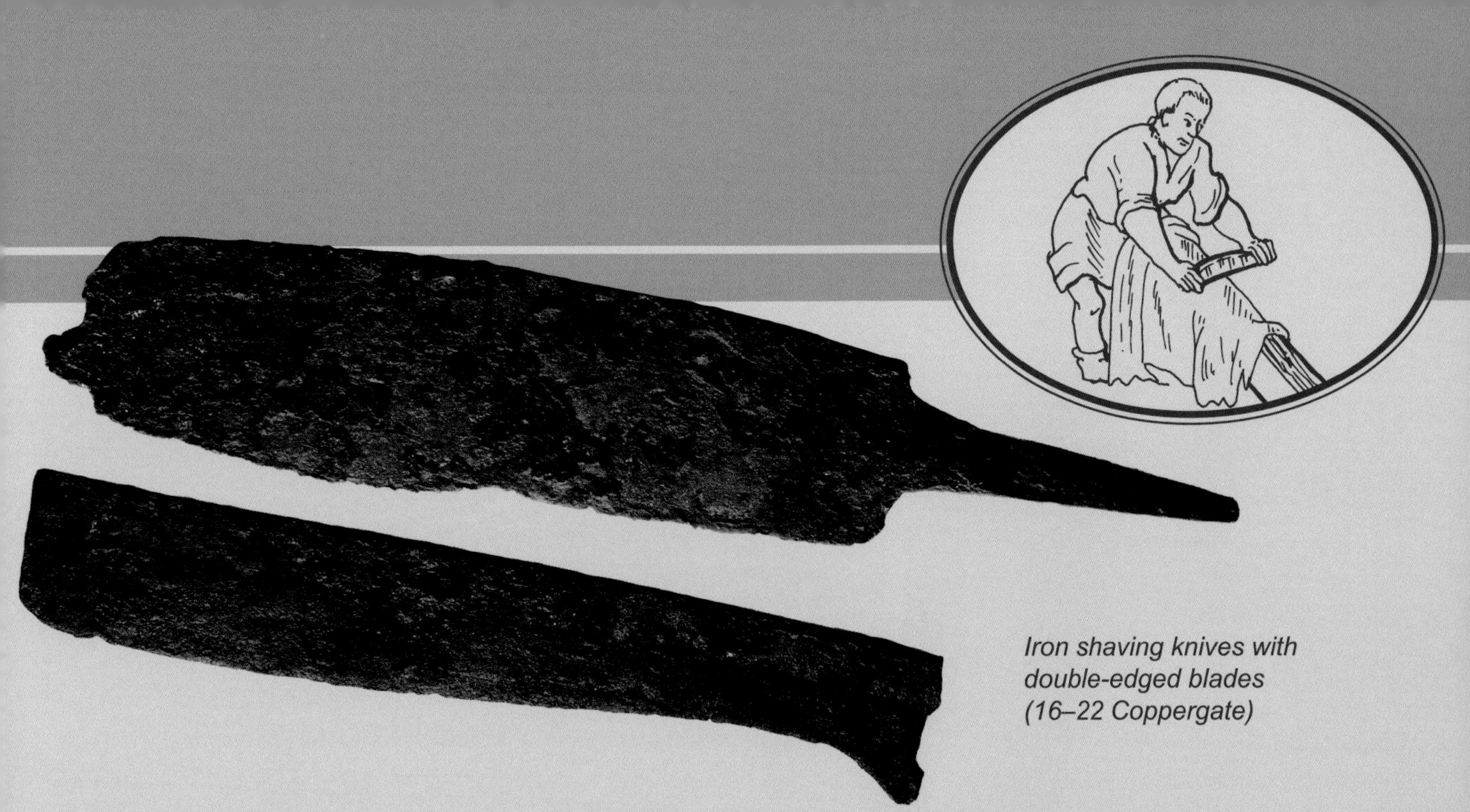

Iron shaving knives with double-edged blades (16–22 Coppergate)

In York, the curriers were among several crafts which carried out ‘tawing’, that is the preparation of other animal skins, such as those of sheep or goats; skinners might also work on these. The barkers were not allowed to prepare these skins, so the curriers received them from the butchers, and undertook the whole process of producing the leather, which might be used to make shoes or saddles.

The Curriers’ Pageant: The Transfiguration

(Pageant 24 of 50)

Jesus and three of his apostles go to a mountain (the Mount of Transfiguration). There, Jesus begins to shine with bright rays of light. Then the prophets Moses and Elijah appear next to him and he speaks with them. Jesus is called ‘Son’ by a voice in the sky, assumed to be God the Father.

The Guild of the

CUTLERS

Iron knife blade inlaid with silver wire (Bedern Foundry)

Leather sheath with detail of impressed decoration (Low Petergate)

The cutlers made, assembled and sold knives and their accessories; they also sold knives imported from elsewhere. The component parts of knives such as the blades, handles and sheaths were made by craftsmen who may have described themselves individually as bladesmiths, hafters or sheathers, but the cutlers' ordinances of 1445 show that all were considered to belong to the craft of cutlers. Moreover, all sellers of knives and sheaths were required to contribute towards the costs of the cutlers' pageant; this indicates that the cutlers were clearly facing competition from other crafts, including the armourers, smiths and mercers.

In York, most cutlers appear to have been concentrated in the area of St Michael-le-Belfrey and Bootham.

Iron knife complete with an ivory socketed handle (46–54 Fishergate)

A bone knife handle plate decorated with tin pins (Bedern Foundry)

The Cutlers' Pageant:
The Conspiracy
(Pageant 28 of 50)

This pageant depicts the conspiracy of the Jews with Pontius Pilate and Judas Iscariot. Following a speech in which Judas explains his motives, he is encountered by a porter, who instinctively recognises Judas' evil nature.

The Guild of the

CORDWAINERS

Cordwainers made all types of new leather boots and shoes, but did not carry out repairs, which was the work of cobblers. The term 'cordwain' derived from the use of fine leather, particularly goatskin, which had been tanned using vegetables, a method developed in Cordoba, Spain; eventually it was applied to any fine leather.

The quality of the leather used to make shoes was very important, because footwear tended to wear out very quickly. The cordwainers used cow leather, and sheep or goat leather provided by the curriers. Regulations decreed that the two different types of leather were not supposed to be used together in one product, nor was one type to be sold deceitfully as the other. Similarly the use of untanned leather, or horse leather, if discovered by searchers, would result in fines.

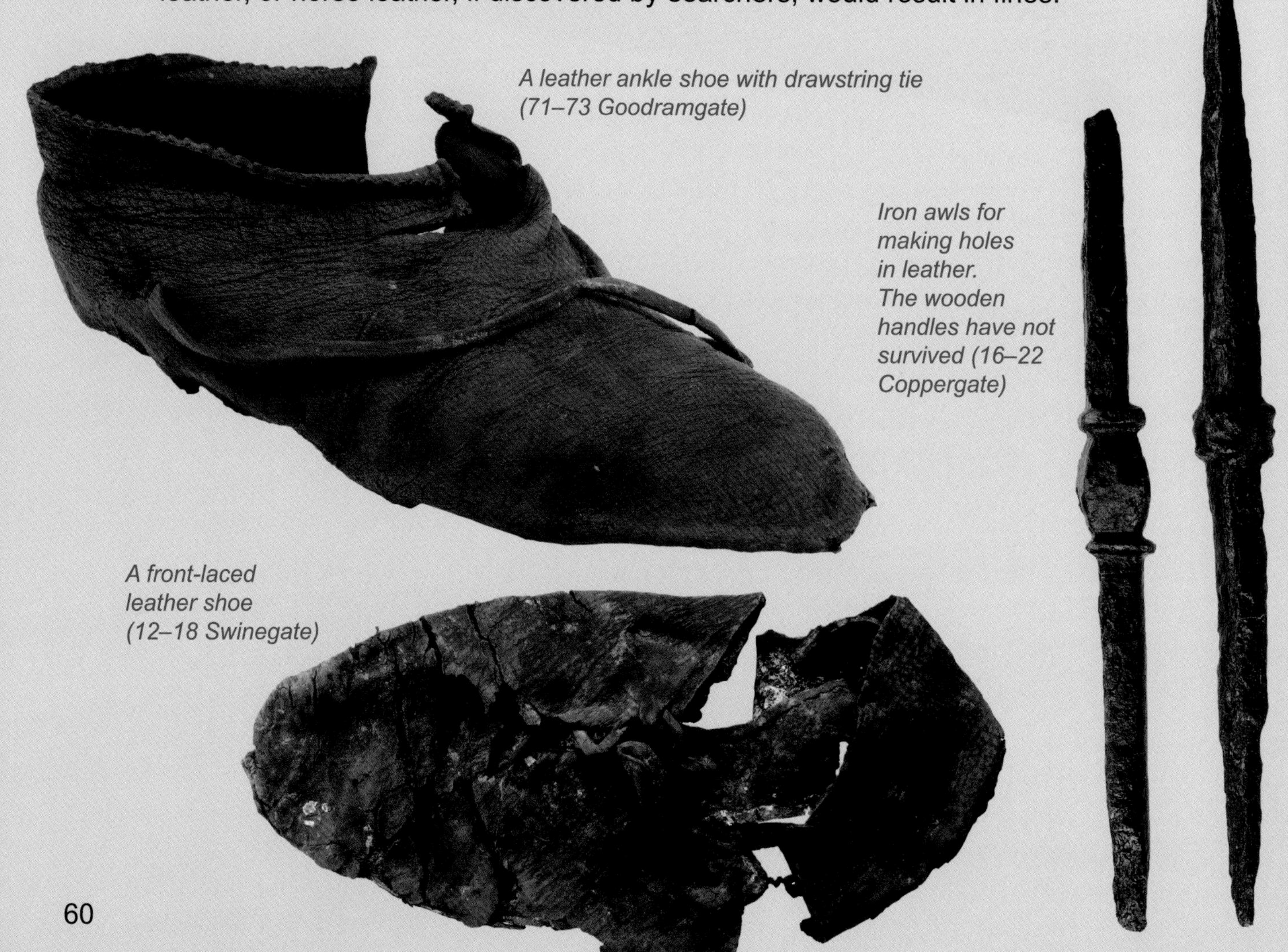

A leather ankle shoe with drawstring tie (71–73 Goodramgate)

Iron awls for making holes in leather. The wooden handles have not survived (16–22 Coppergate)

A front-laced leather shoe (12–18 Swinegate)

An almost complete leather sole, worn through at the big toe (12–18 Swinegate)

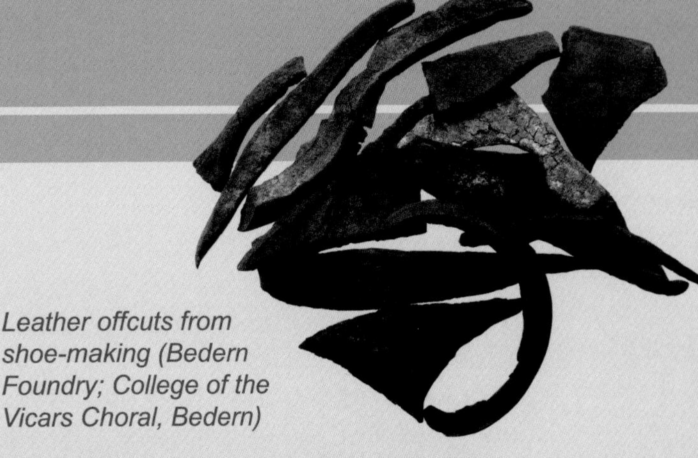

Leather offcuts from shoe-making (Bedern Foundry; College of the Vicars Choral, Bedern)

A study of medieval shoes and offcuts found archaeologically in York reveals that cattle and calf leather was used most in the late 9th to early 11th centuries, after which sheep and goat leather was increasingly employed. During the late 11th to late 13th century, both types of leather were used almost equally, but then cattle leather again became dominant. Until the 15th century, shoe construction generally involved sewing together separately made parts – the main pieces being the sole and the uppers – around a wooden last. Once stitched together, the shoe was turned inside out, protecting and hiding the seams; these shoes are now known as 'turnshoes'.

The Cordwainers' Pageant: The Agony in the Garden and the Betrayal

(Pageant 30 of 50)

Jesus is in the Garden of Gethsemane with three of his disciples to whom he teaches the Lord's Prayer. As he awaits his terrible fate, he begs God to give him strength, and an angel appears. Jesus then predicts that Peter will deny him three times. Meanwhile Judas agrees to betray Jesus, who is then captured.

The cordwainers' pageant incorporated a number of incidents surrounding the capture of Jesus in the Garden of Gethsemane: these included the Vigil of the Apostles, Jesus' prediction of Peter's denials, and the capture of Jesus. For the cordwainers, the most significant event was probably the Vigil of the Apostles – their ordinances forbade them to work at their craft on that particular feast day, and they were also required to maintain a candle in honour of the Vigil of Apostles in one of the city's churches.

The Guild of the

COOKS and WATERLEADERS

The members of the cooks' guild were supposed to have a monopoly in providing food for ceremonies such as feasts, weddings and funerals, but in practice it was impossible to prevent anyone cooking for the public if they chose. Their ordinances of 1424 could only stress that 'the wives of any other artisans should not bake, boil nor roast food in public shops, for sale, unless they are competent to do so'. Apart from cooking meat, the cooks also prepared pies and pasties, jellies, custards and tarts. Regulations controlled the prices they could charge for selling food on the streets. Unfortunately, their interests often overlapped with others in the food provision industry, which caused conflict. One example was the fishmongers; the cooks sold freshwater fish in the city, although their supplies were restricted. When they tried to get around these rules, they were banned from selling fresh fish, and were only allowed to trade in cooked fish.

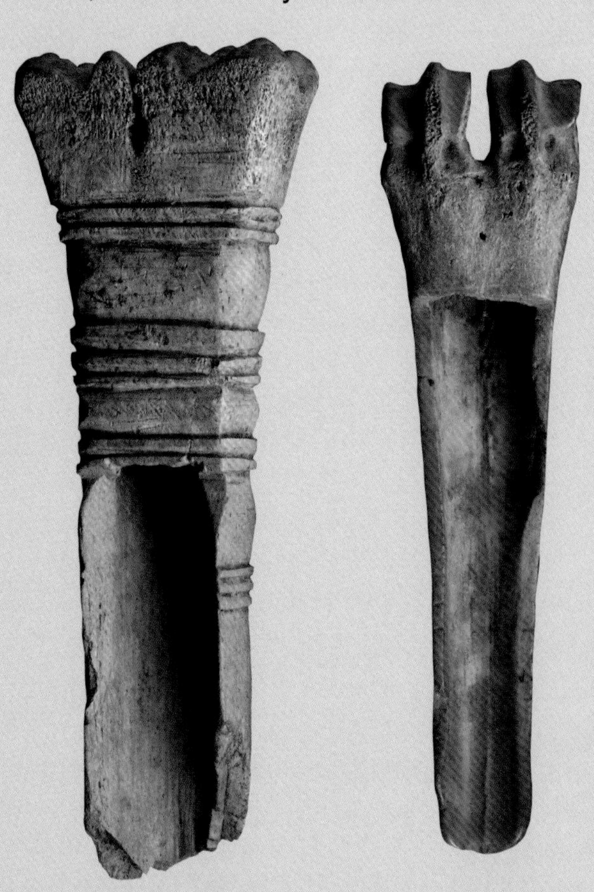

Scoops or apple-corers made of bone (College of the Vicars Choral, Bedern; 1–2 Tower Street)

Part of an iron flesh hook for extracting meat from a cooking pot (College of the Vicars Choral, Bedern)

A miniature version of the sort of copper-alloy cauldron that could have been used by a medieval cook (27 Lawrence Street)

The waterleaders transported water around the city to individual households, probably using leather containers, either carried on yokes across their shoulders, or on horses. Not sufficiently wealthy to put on their own pageant, they shared with others; the Ordo of 1415 reveals that in that year they helped the bakers with the Last Supper pageant, in particular being responsible for Christ washing the disciples' feet. By the third quarter of the 15th century, however, they were working with the cooks.

Cooks' and Waterleaders' Pageant:
The Remorse of Judas

(Pageant 34 of 50)

Pilate asks Caiaphas and Annas, and also his soldiers, about Jesus, and learns that he is in Herod's hands. Judas is full of remorse at his betrayal of Jesus, and begs that Jesus be freed. Despite much pleading, Judas is unable to persuade Pilate to release Jesus, and he throws back the 30 pieces of silver, and plans to kill himself. Pilate tricks a knight into selling him the mount of Calvary.

The Guild of the

PINNERS

In the medieval period, copper-alloy wire pins were used in large numbers as fastenings for clothing and for fixing veils. Made with a wire shank, and another length of wire wrapped around one end to form a head, these pins were typically delicate and light. Vast numbers were often required: Edward III's daughter Princess Joan, for example, who died of plague on her marriage journey in 1348, had 12,000 pins in her trousseau alone. In York, the Pinners' Guild appears to have been established in the mid-14th century, although by 1482–83 the guild had merged with that of the wiredrawers. This was a natural union, as the wiredrawers supplied the wires used by the pinners. Documents indicate that women were sometimes wiredrawers and/or pinners: the widow of York pinner William Couper, for example, retained control of his business on his death in the mid-15th century, and on her own death in 1469 bequeathed materials from the workshop to another woman.

Copper-alloy pins and wires (Hungate)

In 1381, ten pinners are recorded as living in the parish of St Crux, and the area seems to have been a focus for this particular craft. Excavations nearby on Stonebow and Hungate have both provided evidence of pin manufacture from as early as the 14th century, in the form of large quantities of pins and wires, and also of bone tools known as pinners' bones, which were used to hold the pins in place while the tips were being sharpened.

Pinners' bones: the notched ends are thought to have been used to hold the pins in place while the tips were being sharpened (Hungate)

The Pinners' Pageant:
The Crucifixion
(Pageant 37 of 50)

Four soldiers describe their attempts to fix Jesus onto the cross, in graphic and gruesome detail. They struggle to get him into position as they blame poor workmanship and spells cast by Christ for making the job very difficult. The cross is laid on the platform of the wagon with Christ being far less visible to the audience than the soldiers, as he offers his life to save mankind. The soldiers then pull the cross into the upright position, the base dropping into a mortice which has to be wedged. Jesus asks God to forgive the men, who nevertheless continue to mock him and argue over who should have his clothes.

The Guild of the

BUTCHERS

York's butchers worked mainly with cattle, selling not just the cuts of meat, but also the by-products, that is cow and ox hides to the barkers, tallow (animal fat) to the curriers and the chandlers (candle-makers), bones to the pinners and bone-workers, and sheepskins to the curriers and skinners. Butchers often owned their animals and grazing land, but, although many were prosperous individuals, the nature of their occupation, which entailed slaughtering and evisceration, led to the craft being held in contempt. The status of their trade was always perceived to be low, and they were thus considered to be one of the minor crafts in York.

It seems that butchers had begun to congregate around the street now known as The Shambles as early as the 11th century; the shops had slaughterhouses to the rear, and the meat was hung up outside or laid out on 'flesh shamels' (shelves) in front, thus giving the street its current name. At one time the street was known as 'Haymongergate', because the butchers stored fodder for any beasts they kept in stalls before slaughter. The grouping of butchers on this one street is well documented; one record from 1280 lists 17 shops paying a Shamel Tax, a toll which was certainly unpopular. When 14 butchers refused to pay it, the civic authorities punished them by taking 'one knife from each of the aforesaid defendants in the name of distraint for the pence aforesaid being in arrears'; the butchers reacted by taking up 'axes, swords and staves' and recovered their knives the same day.

An iron meat cleaver used to cut joints of meat off a carcass (Hungate)

Waste bones from butchered carcasses, probably produced by slaughterhouses on The Shambles (Hungate)

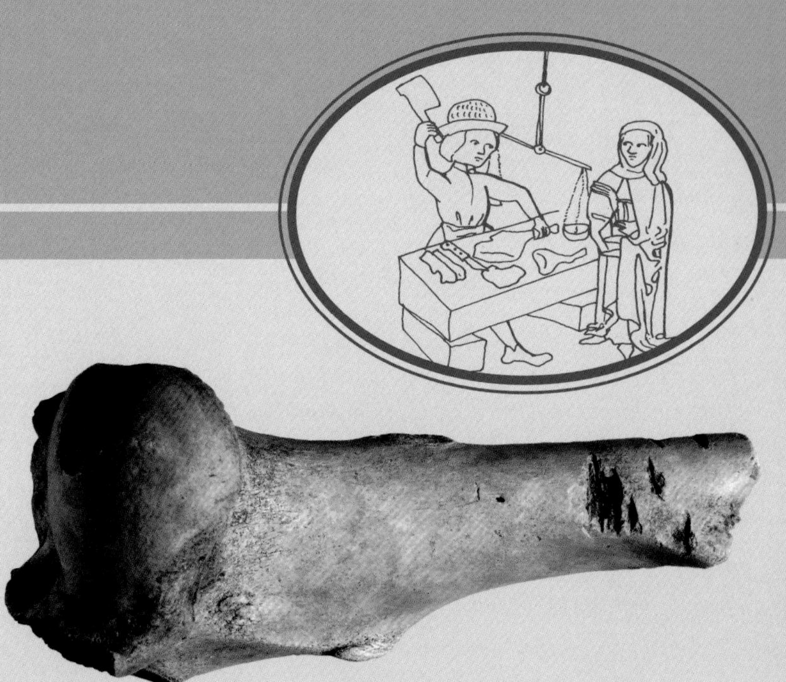

The Butchers' Pageant:
The Death of Christ
(Pageant 38 of 50)

Jesus is on the cross, with the two thieves on either side of him. Mary weeps at the base of the cross for her son, and she is comforted by John. Jesus is very thirsty, and a servant offers him a drink, but it is made of vinegar. Jesus asks God to forgive his tormentors, and commends his spirit to his Father. To ensure Christ is dead, Longinus is instructed to insert his spear into Jesus' side, at which he is miraculously cured of his blindness. Pilate agrees to give Jesus' body to Joseph of Arimathea; together with Nicodemus, he removes Christ's body from the cross, wraps him in a shroud, and anoints him.

Associated so closely with slaughter, there was an obvious logic to the butchers performing this important pageant. In the 14th century, the members of the guild described themselves as 'exposers of flesh for sale', and in this pageant they can be said to kill and expose the flesh of Christ. Moreover, the butchers could easily provide the source of (animal) blood used in the scene where Christ's side is pierced by the blind Longinus. This play features a large cast of characters, which the wealthy butchers would have been able to provide from amongst their ranks.

The Guild of the CARPENTERS

Carpenters were predominantly employed in the construction – and especially the repair – of houses and shops, stables, sheds, and fences, and would have moved from building site to building site as the job required. As most domestic buildings in the city were made almost entirely of wood, these craftsmen would have been kept busy. If local timber was available for use (oak being the most favoured) it would have been selected by the carpenter from a viewing of trees; indeed, carpenters occasionally acted as timber merchants. By the 15th century, however, oak was expensive and York craftsmen became more dependent on cheaper timber imported from the Baltic, and sold on to them by merchants. Timber was also recycled from structures being demolished.

An iron twist auger, complete apart from its wooden handle. This tool acted like a gimlet to start making holes in timber (16–22 Coppergate)

The main tools used were iron axes and adzes for cutting, squaring up and trimming the timbers, and chisels and augers or spoon bits for drilling holes and cutting mortices. Nails were rarely used, mortice-and-tenon joints fixed with wooden pegs being most commonly used for joining timbers. The work was carried out in a framing yard, where timbers would have been laid out, measured and cut to form a pre-fabricated structure. The carpenters made the wooden pegs, and also provided wooden tile pins to the tile thatchers, who used them to peg tiles to the roof.

A structural timber with tool marks in the slot (College of the Vicars Choral, Bedern)

Lead-alloy points used like pencils to mark out setting lines for joints (16–22 Coppergate; College of the Vicars Choral, Bedern)

The carpenters' guild had responsibility not just for the carpenters themselves, but for other specialised wood-workers including sawyers, carvers, joiners and cartwrights. Most were not well off, however, being among the poorest of York's artisans, with even many master carpenters working for a daily wage. Nevertheless, all would have contributed towards the cost of performing the carpenters' pageant.

The Carpenters' Pageant: The Resurrection

(Pageant 40 of 50)

Pilate and his high priests are informed by a centurion that the killing of Jesus has led to unusual natural phenomena, which have persuaded him that Jesus was the Son of God. Pilate orders his soldiers to keep watch at the tomb. An angel shows the three Marys that Jesus is not in the tomb because he has risen, and Mary his mother vows to stay so that she can see him. The soldiers wake up to discover the tomb is empty, and fear Pilate will have them killed for their failing. Upon hearing their tale that they were powerless to prevent Jesus' resurrection, Pilate and his advisers agree that the true story must not be told, and reward the soldiers for promising to tell everyone that Jesus' body was removed by a large force of men, against whom they could not fight.

Despite their apparent lowly status among York's craftsmen, the carpenters' guild was responsible for performing one of the key pageants in the Cycle. This was probably because its origins lay in an early religious guild known as the 'Holy Fraternity of the Resurrection of our Lord'; consequently they performed the pageant on the subject to which their guild was dedicated.

The Guild of the

WOOLPACKERS

For much of the medieval period, wool was the most important commodity in England, whether it was bought and sold as sacks of raw material, or as the cloth that the wool had been woven into. The woolpackers, also described as woolbrokers, were essentially middlemen in the trading of wool; they would advise the producer on prices to be charged, and guarantee the quality of the wool to the purchaser. They might also buy and store wool in anticipation of selling it themselves.

Wooden bale pins, all made of field maple. These fastened the outer wrappings of wool bales or sacks (Carmelite Street)

In the early 14th century, wool merchants from York increasingly became involved in exporting wool; they bought wool from the sheep-farming areas of the North and East Ridings, and exported large amounts via the port at Hull. Exports reached their peak in the later 14th century, with over 1600 sacks of wool shipped out by York merchants in 1378–79, compared with 200 in 1324–25. A sack weighed in the region of 364lb, and would have been made up of approximately 150–200 individual fleeces, so this represents a huge amount of wool. A steady decline in raw wool exports is recorded in the 15th century, however, as wool cloth became a more significant export. The expansion and contraction of the export trade, as well as the more local trade, must have had an impact on the woolpackers, but they were clearly still a wealthy enough guild in the later 15th century to be able to bring forth their pageant.

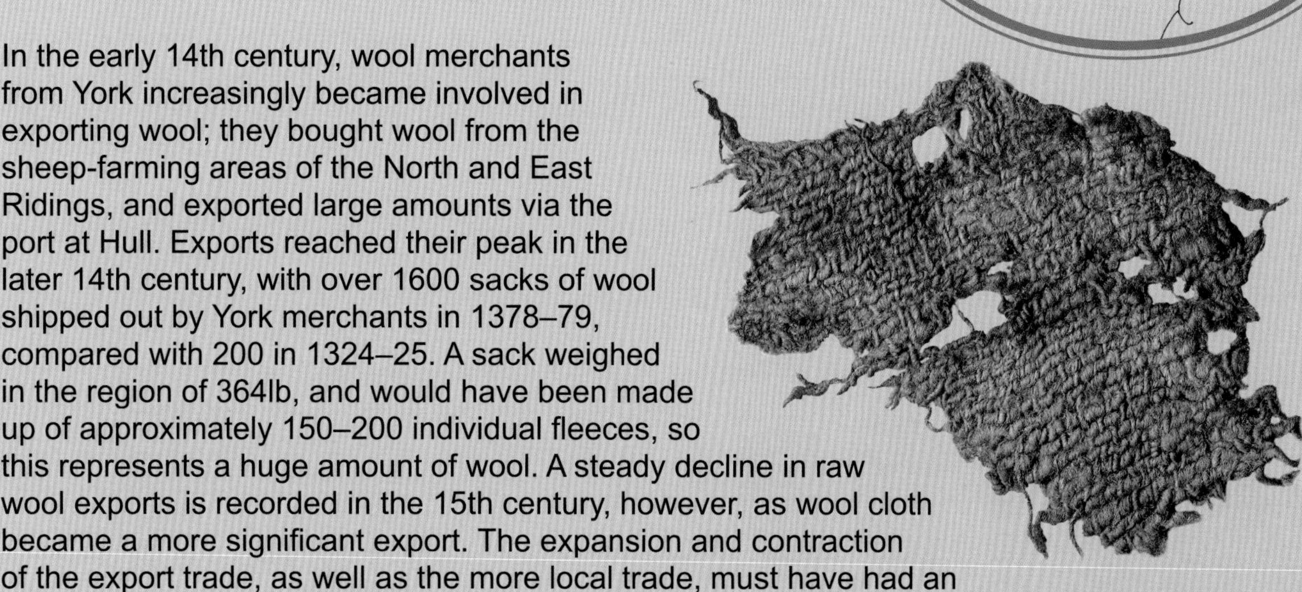

Fragment of woollen cloth (62–68 Low Petergate)

The Woolpackers' Pageant:
The Supper at Emmaus

(Pageant 42 of 50)

Two disciples walking towards Emmaus meet Jesus. They do not recognise him, and discuss their sadness at recent events with him. They persuade him to come and eat with them, and he blesses the meal. They discover he has gone, and realise that their guest was Jesus.

The Guild of the

SCRIVENERS

The guild of scriveners was formed in the 15th century by people who could write and illustrate manuscripts, in particular those who produced legal documents and letters; it evolved over time to include lawyers and accountants. The guild was particularly concerned to establish control over all those writing legal documents, and to ensure their integrity in business, and their competence in practice.

Records relating to the activities of the scriveners of York refer to the production or authentication of administrative and legal documents, and also to members of the guild acting as witnesses to legal documents. John Wodd, a scrivener in the late 15th century, for example, is known to have written many wills.

Evidence of the concern that members of the public could be confident in the services provided by the scriveners is indicated by the oath taken by the members of the London guild from c.1391. In the oath the member must swear to not ‘suffer to be written by none of mine to my power and knowing, any manner of deed or writing to be sealed bearing a date a long time before the making of the same, nor a long time after, nor a blank charter, nor other deed sealed before the writing thereof, nor closed letters of a date far distant, nor of long time where through any falsehood may be perceived in my conscience, nor no copy of a deed but well examined word by word’.

Bone and wood implements with iron tips. These were used either to mark out the positions of the ends of lines on pages of parchment, or to write on wax (1–9 Micklegate; 1–2 Tower Street; 21–33 Aldwark)

A replica of a set of waxed writing tablets found at 12–18 Swinegate

A copper-alloy stylus for writing on wax. The triangular end acted as an eraser (37 Bishophhill Senior)

The Scriveners' Pageant:
The Incredulity of Thomas
(Pageant 43 of 50)

Jesus appears to his disciples after his resurrection but Thomas is absent, and refuses to believe he has risen unless he is able to see Christ for himself, and to see and feel Christ's wounds. Christ appears to Thomas and the other disciples, inviting Thomas to put his hand in to feel the wounds. When Thomas believes, Christ replies that all who believe in his resurrection despite not seeing him will be blessed forever.

The Guild of the

TAILORS

Tailors – or taylors – carried out garment-making of all types for both secular and ecclesiastical customers; these clothes included caps and hoods, hose (leggings and breeches for men), jackets, robes and vestments. As clothes were essential items and in constant demand, tailors were amongst the most numerous of craftsmen. The wealthier tailors tended to be those who dealt in cloth and employed others to do the cutting and sewing, although the Tailors' Ordinances suggest that the most characteristic task of the craft was the cutting of cloth; indeed, the Latin word 'scissor' was the term generally used in documents for a tailor. As with other groups, there was considerable overlap between their products and those of other allied trades, such as the skinners, hosiers and cappers. Dealing in cloth also brought them into competition with the drapers, who were specialised cloth merchants.

In the medieval period, the tailors were associated with the religious and charitable confraternity of St John the Baptist, which built the hall now known as the Merchant Taylors' Hall, but which was called St John the Baptist's Hall until the late 16th century. By this time, the tailors had officially merged with the drapers and hosiers. The Company of the Merchant Taylors was officially recognised by a royal charter in 1662.

Iron and copper-alloy needles (16–22 Coppergate)

Copper-alloy thimbles: the larger thimble has a separate leather lining or padding (College of the Vicars Choral, Bedern; 46–54 Fishergate)

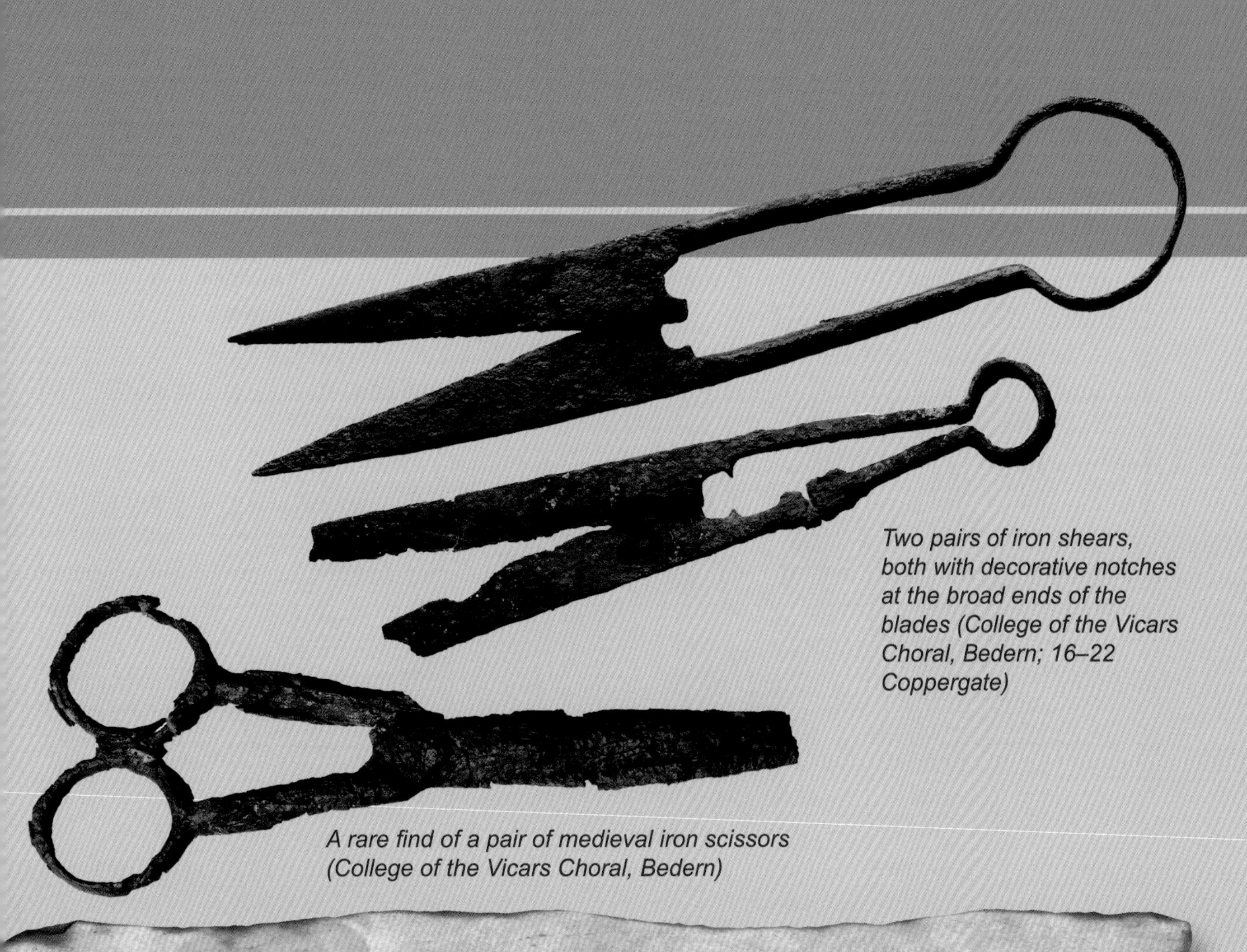

Two pairs of iron shears, both with decorative notches at the broad ends of the blades (College of the Vicars Choral, Bedern; 16–22 Coppergate)

A rare find of a pair of medieval iron scissors (College of the Vicars Choral, Bedern)

The Tailors' Pageant:
The Ascension
(Pageant 44 of 50)

Forty days after his resurrection, Jesus appears to Mary and his disciples. He tells them he will return at Doomsday to judge all men, to whom he instructs the apostles to go out and to teach the gospel. He ascends into heaven as an angel sings, and his followers go off to spread Christ's message.

For the performers of this pageant, representing the ascension into heaven on a wagon in the city streets must have posed a great challenge; an image of Christ may have been drawn up on pulleys to depict the scene.

Further information about the illustrated objects

Page	Guild	Object	Site Name	Small Find No(s)	Location of Object
4		Seal matrix	62–68 Low Petergate	809	YAT
4		Cloth seal	Judges Lodging, Lendal	34	YAT
5		Cloth seal	Skeldergate, Pawsons Warehouse	2005	YAT
6		Leather offcuts	College of the Vicars Choral, Bedern (1973.13)	1647	YAT
6		Sheath	12–18 Swinegate	250	YAT
7		Architectural fragment	Hungate	AF174	YAT
13		Bones	118–126 Walmgate	1097	YAT
28	Barkers	Bark rolls	16–22 Coppergate	102	YAT
30	Coopers	Bucket	16–22 Coppergate	4176	YAT
31	Coopers	Caskhead	Bedern Foundry	1778	YAT
32	Armourers	Scabbard fragment	12–18 Swinegate	500	YAT
33	Armourers	Chain Mail	16–22 Coppergate	2668	YAT
33	Armourers	Chain mail on pottery	1-9 Bridge Street	18	YAT
33	Armourers	Finger joint covers	16–22 Coppergate	2844, 2845	YAT
34	Shipwrights	Clench bolts	16–22 Coppergate	816, 1018, 1145, 1176	YAT
35	Shipwrights	Boat timber fragment	Coppergate Watching Brief	(Timber) 71	YAT
37	Fishers	Fish hooks	16–22 Coppergate	1397, 1683	YAT
37	Fishers	Net weight	16–22 Coppergate	4968	YAT
37	Fishers	Net sinkers	46–54 Fishergate	5393, 6403, 6823, 7805	YAT
38	Pewterers	Chalice and paten	46–54 Fishergate	5712	YAT
39	Pewterers	Small object moulds	College of the Vicars Choral, Bedern (1973.13)	778, 2628	YAT
40	Pewterers	Ampulla	Hungate	4039	YAT
40	Pewterers	Ampulla mould	34 Shambles	3	YAT
41	Pewterers	Mount	City Mills, Skeldergate	442	YAT
41	Pewterers	Vessel mould fragment	Bedern Foundry	3061	YAT
43	Tile Thatchers	Ladder upright	16–22 Coppergate	16254	YAT
44	Goldsmiths	Gold finger ring	College of the Vicars Choral, Bedern (1976.14)	390	YM

Page	Guild	Object	Site Name	Small Find No(s)	Location of Object
44	Goldsmiths	Gold finger ring	16–22 Coppergate	872	YM
44	Goldsmiths	Gold brooch	Merchant Adventurers' Hall	4	Merchant Adventurers' Hall
45	Goldsmiths	Gold brooch	College of the Vicars Choral, Bedern (1973.13)	2847	YM
45	Goldsmiths	Gold wire	24–30 Tanner Row	1018	YAT
46	Masons	Column base	College of the Vicars Choral, Bedern (1973.13)	AF9051	YAT
47	Masons	Mason's pickaxe	Bedern Foundry	1592	YAT
48	Marshals	Fleam	16–22 Coppergate	1848	YAT
48,49	Marshals	Horseshoes	16–22 Coppergate	1003, 1967, 516	YAT
50	Girdlers	Girdle	16–22 Coppergate	3006	YAT
50	Girdlers	Harness	Bedern Foundry	2101	YAT
50	Girdlers	Girdle	Bedern Foundry	1747	YAT
51	Girdlers	Dog-collar?	16–22 Coppergate	842	YAT
51	Girdlers	Sheath chape	16–22 Coppergate	2544	YAT
51	Girdlers	Sheath chape	46–54 Fishergate	100	YAT
51	Girdlers	Belt mount	Bedern Foundry	924	YAT
51	Girdlers	Belt mounts	College of the Vicars Choral, Bedern (1973.13)	2202, 2278	YAT
52	Spurriers	Rowel spur	30 Aldwark	1	YAT
52	Spurriers	Rowel spur	College of the Vicars Choral, Bedern (1973.13)	2446	YAT
52	Spurriers	Prick spur	1–2 Tower Street	500	YAT
53	Lorimer	Horse bit	16–22 Coppergate	1281	YAT
54	Smiths	Pickaxe head	62–68 Low Petergate	744	YAT
54	Smiths	Metal-working tongs	46–54 Fishergate	3856	YAT
54	Smiths	Metal-working tongs	Bedern Foundry	2070	YAT
54	Smiths	Metal-working punch	16–22 Coppergate	2234	YAT
54	Smiths	Metal-working punch	46–54 Fishergate	621	YAT
55	Smiths	Padlock keys	16–22 Coppergate	1617, 2390, 4116, 4873	YAT
55	Smiths	Barrel padlock	16–22 Coppergate	2982	YAT
56	Curriers	Shavings	16–22 Coppergate	17446	YAT

Page	Guild	Object	Site Name	Small Find No(s)	Location of Object
57	Curriers	Curriers' knives	16–22 Coppergate	3603, 4985	YAT
58	Cutlers	Inlaid knife	College of the Vicars Choral, Bedern (1976.14)	5133	YAT
58	Cutlers	Sheath	62–68 Low Petergate	294	YAT
59	Cutlers	Knife	46–54 Fishergate	4945	YAT
59	Cutlers	Knife handle	Bedern Foundry	1558	YAT
60	Cordwainers	Shoe	71–73 Goodramgate	31	YAT
60	Cordwainers	Awls	16–22 Coppergate	940, 2228	YAT
60,61	Cordwainers	Shoes	12–18 Swinegate	208, 266	YAT
61	Cordwainers	Offcuts	Bedern Foundry	1640, 1647	YAT
61	Cordwainers	Offcuts	College of the Vicars Choral, Bedern (1973.13)	2079	YAT
62	Cooks	Bone scoop	College of the Vicars Choral, Bedern (1973.13)	2129	YAT
62	Cooks	Bone scoop	1–2 Tower Street	142	YAT
62	Cooks	Flesh hook	College of the Vicars Choral, Bedern (1973.13)	2090	YAT
63	Cooks	Miniature cauldron	27 Lawrence Street	46	YAT
64	Pinners	Pins/wires	Hungate	677	YAT
64	Pinners	Pins	Hungate	10330	YAT
65	Pinners	Pinners' bones	Hungate	108, 110, 3110, 4013, 6184	YAT
66	Butchers	Cleaver	Hungate	6336	YAT
67	Butchers	Animal bones	Hungate		YAT
68	Carpenters	Auger	16–22 Coppergate	1561	YAT
68	Carpenters	Lead point	16–22 Coppergate	3184	YAT
68	Carpenters	Lead points	College of the Vicars Choral, Bedern (1976.14)	2794, 2799	YAT
68	Carpenters	Lead point	College of the Vicars Choral, Bedern (1976.14)	906	YAT
70	Woolpackers	Bale pins	Carmelite Street	84	YAT
71	Woolpackers	Textile fragment	62–68 Low Petergate	318	YAT
72	Scriveners	Parchment pricker	1–9 Micklegate	70	YAT
72	Scriveners	Parchment prickers	1–2 Tower Street	281, 468, 621	YAT

Page	Guild	Object	Site Name	Small Find No(s)	Location of Object
72	Scriveners	Parchment pricker	Ebor Brewery, 21–33 Aldwark	943	YAT
73	Scriveners	Stylus	37 Bishophill Senior	129	YAT
73	Scriveners	Waxed tablets	12–18 Swinegate	257	YAT
74	Tailors	Thimble	46–54 Fishergate	2248	YAT
74	Tailors	Needles	16–22 Coppergate	399, 901, 933	YAT
74	Tailors	Thimble	College of the Vicars Choral, Bedern (1973.13)	2063	YAT
74	Tailors	Thimble	46–54 Fishergate	2248	YAT
75	Tailors	Scissors	College of the Vicars Choral, Bedern (1973.13)	2483	YAT
75	Tailors	Shears	16–22 Coppergate	1387	YAT
75	Tailors	Shears	College of the Vicars Choral, Bedern (1973.13)	2164	YAT

Locations:
YAT = York Archaeological Trust
YM = Yorkshire Museum

Acknowledgements

This book was written by Nicola Rogers, but draws heavily upon work carried out by York Archaeological Trust staff, past and present, between 1972 and 2012, which the author acknowledges with gratitude.

Particular thanks go to Dr Ailsa Mainman, Dr Richard Hall, Ian Panter, Kate Kenward, Mags Felter, Christine Kyriacou, Rachel Cubitt, Christine McDonnell, Geoff Krause, Dr Jayne Rimmer, Clare Rainsford, Dr Kate Giles, and Dr Sarah Rees-Jones.

Design and layout by Lesley Collett, and editing by Frances Mee. Photographs have been taken by Mike Andrews, Jon Brownridge, Lesley Collett and other YAT photographers.

Further Reading

P. V. Addyman (ed.), *The Archaeology of York,* Vol.17, parts 1–16, The Small Finds
R. Beadle and P. M. King, *York Mystery Plays. A Selection in Modern Spelling* (1984, reissued 2009)
J. Blair and N. Ramsay (eds.), *English Medieval Industries* (1991)
G. Dean, *Medieval York* (2008)
R. A. Hall, *English Heritage Book of York* (1996)
C. Kyriacou, F. Mee and N. Rogers, *Treasures of York* (2004)
H. Swanson, *Medieval Artisans* (1989)